Discipline of a Godly Father

Biblical Principles for Raising Children
and Leaving a Lasting Legacy

By
Ethan Shepherd

Copyright © 2025

By
Ethan Shepherd

All rights reserved. No part of this publication may be reproduced, distributed, or transmitted in any form or by any means, including photocopying, recording, or other electronic or mechanical methods, without the prior written permission of the publisher, except in the case of brief quotations embodied in critical reviews and certain other noncommercial uses permitted by copyright law

Table of Content

Introduction 6
The Call to Godly Fatherhood 6
    Understanding the Role of a Godly Father 7
    Why Biblical Discipline Matters 9
    The Power of a Father's Legacy 10
Chapter 1 13
Foundations of a Godly Father 13
    The Biblical Model of Fatherhood 14
    A Father's Role as Priest, Provider, and Protector 20
    Leading by Example: Walking in Faith 24
Chapter 2 28
The Heart of Discipline 28
    What Is Biblical Discipline? 28
    The Difference Between Discipline and Punishment 33
    Teaching with Love, Not Fear 37
Chapter 3 41
Training Up a Child in the Way of the Lord 41
    Instilling Christian Values from an Early Age 42
    The Power of Daily Devotions and Prayer 49
    Raising Children with Integrity and Character 52
Chapter 4 57
Leading with Love and Authority 57
    The Balance Between Grace and Discipline 58
    Correcting with Patience and Wisdom 64
    The Role of Encouragement and Affirmation 67
Chapter 5 72
Building Strong Family Relationships 72

Being Present: The Gift of Time.................................... 72
Creating a Christ-Centered Home................................. 79
The Importance of Open Communication...................... 84

Chapter 6 89
Overcoming Challenges in Fatherhood 89
Handling Disobedience with Wisdom............................. 90
Dealing with the Influence of Culture and Media........... 96
Strengthening Faith During Difficult Times................... 100

Chapter 7 105
Teaching Responsibility and Hard Work 105
Instilling a Strong Work Ethic in Children.................... 106
Biblical Lessons on Stewardship and Money Management 113
Preparing Kids for Adulthood with Life Skills.............. 116

Chapter 8 121
Passing Down a Legacy of Faith 121
The Impact of a Father's Example................................. 122
How to Leave a Spiritual Inheritance............................. 128
Raising the Next Generation of Godly Leaders............. 133

Conclusion 137
Embracing Your Role as a Godly Father 137
Reflecting on the Journey of Fatherhood....................... 137
Committing to a Lifetime of Faithful Parenting............ 140
Trusting God in Every Step... 142
Final Words: The Reward of Faithful Fatherhood......... 144

Introduction

The Call to Godly Fatherhood

Fatherhood is one of the greatest callings a man can receive. It is not merely about providing for a child's physical needs but about shaping their spiritual and moral foundation. The role of a godly father is a divine assignment—one that requires faith, wisdom, patience, and unwavering commitment.

In today's world, fatherhood is under attack. Society often downplays the importance of fathers, portraying them as dispensable or secondary figures in a child's development. However, Scripture makes it clear that a father's role is not only essential but also a reflection of God's own heart. A godly father is called to be a leader, teacher, protector, and role model for his children, demonstrating Christ's love through his actions, discipline, and guidance.

The responsibility of raising godly children is not easy, but it is a journey filled with purpose. A father who embraces his calling with faith and obedience will leave a lasting legacy—not just for his children but for generations to come. This book is a guide for Christian fathers who desire to raise their children in the ways of the Lord, instilling biblical discipline, integrity, and strong moral values that will endure the test of time.

Understanding the Role of a Godly Father

Fatherhood is more than a biological connection; it is a sacred duty entrusted to men by God. From the very beginning, God designed fathers to play a crucial role in the spiritual and emotional development of their children. In **Deuteronomy 6:6-7**, God commands fathers to teach His laws diligently to their children, instructing them in His ways at all times.

A godly father is called to fulfill three primary roles in his child's life:

1. Priest

A godly father serves as the spiritual leader of his home. He is responsible for leading his family in prayer, studying the Word of God, and setting an example of faith. His children should see him actively seeking God's presence, not just in church but in everyday life. By doing so, he creates an environment where faith is nurtured and where children grow up knowing and trusting in God.

2. Provider

Provision goes beyond financial support. While it is important for a father to provide for his family's physical needs, his role as a provider also includes emotional, psychological, and spiritual nourishment. A godly father provides love, security, guidance, and wisdom. He instills confidence in his children by affirming their worth and teaching them the importance of faith, hard work, and responsibility.

3. Protector

A father is called to be a shield for his children—protecting them not just from physical dangers but from spiritual and moral corruption. In a world filled with harmful influences, a godly father guards his children's hearts and minds, teaching them to discern right from wrong and to make choices that honor God. His discipline, guidance, and involvement in their lives create a foundation of security and stability.

The role of a godly father is a high calling that requires intentionality. It is not about being perfect but about being present, engaged, and committed to raising children who love and follow God.

Why Biblical Discipline Matters

Discipline is a word that often carries a negative connotation in today's culture, where many view it as harsh or unnecessary. However, biblical discipline is an act of love, not punishment. It is about teaching and training children in the ways of the Lord so they can grow into responsible, God-fearing adults.

Proverbs 22:6 reminds us, *"Train up a child in the way he should go, and when he is old, he will not depart from it."* This verse emphasizes that discipline is not about control but about guidance—leading children onto the right path so they can walk in wisdom and righteousness.

Biblical Discipline vs. Worldly Discipline

The world often promotes permissive parenting, where children are given free rein without correction, leading to entitlement, lack of respect, and moral confusion. However, biblical discipline teaches that correction is a necessary part of love. **Hebrews 12:6** says, *"For whom the Lord loves He chastens, and scourges every son* *whom He receives."* If God Himself disciplines those He loves, then earthly fathers must follow His example.

Biblical discipline includes:

- **Teaching with love and patience** – Not reacting out of anger but correcting with wisdom.
- **Setting clear boundaries** – Helping children understand the consequences of their actions.
- **Encouraging responsibility** – Teaching children to take ownership of their choices.
- **Fostering self-control** – Guiding them to develop discipline in their thoughts, words, and actions.

A father who disciplines biblically raises children who are not only well-mannered but also spiritually strong. Discipline, when done with love, builds confidence, character, and respect for authority—qualities that will benefit children throughout their lives.

The Power of a Father's Legacy

A father's impact extends far beyond his lifetime. The values he instills, the faith he demonstrates, and the love he shows create a legacy that will influence generations. Children often carry the lessons they learn from their fathers into their own families, shaping the next wave of godly men and women.

1. The Influence of a Godly Father

Studies show that fathers who are actively involved in their children's spiritual and emotional development significantly impact their future success, faith, and well-being. A child who sees his father consistently seeking God, treating others with kindness, and standing firm in biblical principles is more likely to adopt those values.

Psalm 103:17-18 states, *"But the mercy of the Lord is from everlasting to everlasting on those who fear Him, and His righteousness to children's children, to such as keep His covenant, and to those who remember His commandments to do them."* This means that a godly father's obedience to God creates blessings that extend beyond his own life.

2. What Legacy Will You Leave?

Every father leaves behind a legacy—whether good or bad. The question is, what kind of legacy are you building? Will your children remember you as a man of faith, integrity, and love? Will they see the power of God reflected in your actions?

A father's legacy is not built in a single moment but in the daily decisions he makes. By choosing to walk in faith, lead with love, and discipline with wisdom, a godly father lays the foundation for a future filled with God's blessings.

Final Thoughts

The journey of fatherhood is one of the most rewarding yet challenging responsibilities a man can undertake. But you are not alone. God has given fathers the wisdom of His Word and the guidance of His Spirit to navigate this sacred calling.

As you read through this book, I encourage you to embrace your role with humility and dedication. Learn from the examples in Scripture, apply biblical principles to your parenting, and trust God to shape you into the father He has called you to be.

Your children are watching, learning, and growing under your influence. What you do today will echo in their lives for years to come. Take up the call to godly fatherhood, discipline with love, and leave a legacy that honors God.

Chapter 1

Foundations of a Godly Father

Fatherhood is more than a biological function; it is a divine calling that carries immense responsibility. A godly father is not merely someone who provides for his children's material needs but someone who actively shapes their spiritual and moral character. The way a father leads, loves, and disciplines his children has far-reaching consequences, influencing not only their lives but also future generations.

The foundation of godly fatherhood is rooted in Scripture. Throughout the Bible, God has provided a clear model for how fathers should nurture, instruct, and guide their children. Without this foundation, fatherhood becomes a role filled with uncertainty and inconsistency. But with it, a man can fulfill his calling with confidence, wisdom, and purpose.

In this chapter, we will explore what it means to be a godly father and examine the biblical model of fatherhood that God has laid out for us.

The Biblical Model of Fatherhood

To understand what it means to be a godly father, we must first look to the ultimate example—God Himself. The Bible repeatedly refers to God as our Father, demonstrating His love, guidance, discipline, and provision for His children. As earthly fathers, we are called to reflect these same qualities in our own parenting.

1. A Father Who Loves Unconditionally

One of the most defining characteristics of God as our Father is His unconditional love. He does not love us based on our performance but rather because we are His children.

Romans 8:38-39 says:
"For I am convinced that neither death nor life, neither angels nor demons, neither the present nor the future, nor any powers, neither height nor depth, nor anything else in all creation, will be able to separate us from the love of God that is in Christ Jesus our Lord."

A godly father follows this example by showing his children that his love is not based on conditions, accomplishments, or failures. Many children struggle with insecurity because they feel they must earn their father's love through achievements. But when a father models God's love, his children grow up with confidence, knowing they are valued not for what they do but for who they are.

This kind of love does not mean overlooking mistakes or avoiding discipline. Instead, it means that even in correction, a father reassures his children that his love remains unchanged.

2. A Father Who Leads by Example

God does not simply tell us how to live—He shows us. Jesus Christ, God's Son, lived a perfect life on earth, demonstrating what it means to walk in righteousness. Likewise, a godly father must lead his children not just with words but with actions.

1 Corinthians 11:1 says:
"Follow my example, as I follow the example of Christ."

Children learn more from what they see than from what they hear. A father who teaches biblical principles but does not live by them sends mixed signals. If a father expects his children to be honest but engages in dishonesty, they will adopt what they see rather than what they are told.

A godly father models integrity, humility, faithfulness, and perseverance. He teaches his children how to pray not just by instructing them but by letting them see him in prayer. He demonstrates respect for others, kindness, and generosity through his own actions. His life serves as a blueprint for his children to follow.

3. A Father Who Provides and Protects

In **Matthew 7:9-11**, Jesus says:
"Which of you, if your son asks for bread, will give him a stone? Or if he asks for a fish, will give him a snake? If you, then, though you are evil, know how to give good gifts to your children, how much more will your Father in heaven give good gifts to those who ask him!"

God provides for our needs, and in the same way, earthly fathers are responsible for providing for their families. This provision is not just financial—it includes emotional security, wisdom, and guidance.

A godly father ensures that his home is a place of safety and stability. He protects his children from harm—whether it be physical, emotional, or spiritual. In today's world, children are exposed to many harmful influences, from toxic entertainment to ungodly ideologies. A father must be vigilant, setting boundaries and teaching his children how to discern what is right and wrong.

4. A Father Who Disciplines with Love

Discipline is an essential aspect of fatherhood. It is not about punishment but about correction and training.

Hebrews 12:6 says:
"The Lord disciplines those He loves, and He chastens everyone He accepts as His son."

A godly father does not discipline out of anger or frustration but out of love and a desire to guide his children in the right direction. His correction is not meant to break their spirit but to strengthen their character.

Discipline should always be fair, consistent, and accompanied by an explanation. When a father takes the time to explain why certain behaviors are wrong and offers guidance on making better choices, his children will respect his authority and grow in wisdom.

5. A Father Who Encourages and Affirms

Just as God speaks words of blessing and encouragement over His children, a godly father should do the same. Words have the power to shape a child's identity and future.

Proverbs 18:21 says:
"The tongue has the power of life and death, and those who love it will eat its fruit."

A godly father speaks life into his children. He affirms their worth, encourages their efforts, and reminds them of God's plans for their lives. When a father consistently builds up his children with words of love, wisdom, and faith, they grow up with confidence and a strong sense of identity in Christ.

6. A Father Who Prays for His Children

Perhaps one of the most powerful things a father can do for his children is to pray for them. A godly father recognizes that he cannot control every aspect of his child's life, but he can commit them into God's hands.

Job 1:5 tells us that Job regularly prayed for his children, offering sacrifices on their behalf. This shows a father's role as a spiritual intercessor for his family.

A father's prayers can:

- Protect his children from harm.
- Guide them in making wise decisions.
- Strengthen their faith in God.
- Cover their future, including their careers, marriages, and spiritual growth.

When children see their father praying for them, it instills in them the importance of a personal relationship with God.

Final Thoughts

A godly father is a man who understands that his role is not just about authority but about servanthood. He mirrors God's love, leads by example, provides for and protects his children, disciplines with wisdom, speaks words of encouragement, and prays diligently for his family.

The biblical model of fatherhood is not an impossible standard—it is a divine blueprint that every man can strive toward with God's help. No father is perfect, but with a heart surrendered to God, he can build a legacy of faith, strength, and godliness that will impact generations to come.

As you continue reading, remember that God has entrusted you with this sacred responsibility. Embrace it with faith, and rely on Him to shape you into the father He has called you to be.

A Father's Role as Priest, Provider, and Protector

Fatherhood is a divine assignment that extends beyond biological responsibility. It is a role ordained by God, requiring a man to lead, nurture, and defend his family spiritually, emotionally, and physically. In the biblical model of fatherhood, a godly father functions as a **priest**, a **provider**, and a **protector** within his home.

1. The Father as the Priest of the Home

In the Old Testament, priests were responsible for offering sacrifices, interceding for the people, and teaching the Word of God. Similarly, a father serves as the spiritual leader of his home, standing in the gap for his family through prayer, teaching, and godly example.

Job 1:5 tells us that Job would wake up early in the morning to offer sacrifices on behalf of his children, thinking, *"Perhaps my children have sinned and cursed God in their hearts."* Job's example shows a father's duty to intercede for his children, covering them in prayer and leading them in righteousness.

A godly father acts as a priest by:

- **Teaching the Word of God** – *Deuteronomy 6:6-7* instructs fathers to impress God's

commandments upon their children, discussing them daily.
- **Praying for and with his family** – Leading by example, a father should make prayer a central part of family life.
- **Encouraging faith in Christ** – A father's role is not just to know God but to help his family cultivate a personal relationship with Him.

A father who fails in his priestly role leaves a spiritual gap in his home, exposing his children to worldly influences without godly guidance. He must take responsibility for ensuring that his household follows the Lord.

Practical Ways to Fulfill the Role of a Priest

- Establish daily or weekly family devotions.
- Pray for and with your children, teaching them to rely on God.
- Model a life of obedience and trust in God.
- Lead your family in attending church and serving in ministry.

2. The Father as a Provider

Provision is not merely about finances; it encompasses everything a family needs to thrive—physically, emotionally, and spiritually.

Physical Provision

A father must ensure that his family has shelter, food, and security. **1 Timothy 5:8** says, *"Anyone who does not provide for their relatives, and especially for their own household, has denied the faith and is worse than an unbeliever."* This verse highlights the importance of a father's responsibility to work diligently to support his family.

However, provision is not just about working hard but also about teaching financial wisdom. A godly father helps his children understand the value of hard work, stewardship, and generosity. He sets an example by managing finances wisely, avoiding unnecessary debt, and being generous to those in need.

Emotional Provision

Many fathers provide financially but neglect their children emotionally. A godly father creates a safe environment where his children feel loved, heard, and valued. He listens attentively, offers encouragement, and affirms his children's worth.

Spiritual Provision

A father provides for his family's spiritual well-being by ensuring that his home is built on biblical principles. He leads his family in worship, teaches them God's word, and ensures they have an environment where faith can flourish.

3. The Father as a Protector

A father's role as protector extends beyond physical security. He is also responsible for shielding his family from emotional and spiritual harm.

Physical Protection

A father should ensure that his family is safe from harm. This includes being mindful of their physical environment, knowing who influences them, and teaching them how to make wise decisions regarding their safety.

Emotional Protection

Children thrive when they feel emotionally safe. A godly father creates a home where his children are free to express themselves, knowing they will be treated with love and respect. He avoids harsh criticism and instead disciplines with love and patience.

Spiritual Protection

A godly father protects his children from harmful influences by being vigilant about the content they consume, the friendships they build, and the values they adopt. **Proverbs 4:23** says, *"Above all else, guard your heart, for everything you do flows from it."* A father helps his children guard their hearts by teaching them biblical principles and helping them discern right from wrong.

Practical Ways to Fulfill the Role of a Protector

- Be present and involved in your children's lives.
- Set clear moral boundaries in the home.
- Teach your children how to recognize and resist negative influences.
- Provide wise counsel when your children face difficult decisions.

Leading by Example: Walking in Faith

A father cannot expect his children to follow God if he himself is not walking in faith. The most effective way to lead is by example.

1. The Power of Example

Children learn by watching. A father who models integrity, humility, and faithfulness teaches his children more than a thousand lectures ever could.

Joshua 24:15 says, *"As for me and my household, we will serve the Lord."* Joshua took personal responsibility for his family's faith. Likewise, a godly father sets the spiritual tone for his home.

A Godly Father Walks in Integrity

Integrity means doing what is right even when no one is watching. A godly father's life should be consistent, whether at home, work, or church. His children should see the same character in him at all times.

A Godly Father Walks in Humility

Being a leader does not mean being domineering. Jesus, the greatest leader of all time, modeled servant leadership. **Philippians 2:3-4** says, *"Do nothing out of selfish ambition or vain conceit. Rather, in humility value others above yourselves, not looking to your own interests but each of you to the interests of the others."*

A godly father leads by serving his family—helping with tasks, listening to their concerns, and putting their needs before his own.

A Godly Father Walks in Faithfulness

Faithfulness means being reliable, trustworthy, and committed. A father who is faithful in his marriage, work, and spiritual life sets a strong example for his children.

2. Teaching by Doing

A father who prays daily shows his children the importance of prayer. A father who reads the Bible consistently teaches his children that God's Word is a priority. A father who remains faithful to his commitments teaches his children the value of integrity.

Practical Steps to Lead by Example

- Let your children see you reading the Bible and praying.
- Be honest in all dealings, even when it's inconvenient.
- Apologize when you make mistakes to show humility.
- Show kindness, patience, and forgiveness in everyday life.

Final Thoughts

A godly father lays the foundation for his children's spiritual, emotional, and physical well-being. He serves as a **priest, provider, and protector**, ensuring that his home is a place where faith thrives. More importantly, he leads by **example**, walking in faith, integrity, humility, and righteousness.

Fatherhood is not just about authority—it is about responsibility. It is about shaping lives, influencing generations, and leaving a legacy that reflects God's love and truth. As a father, your impact goes beyond what you say; it is seen in what you do.

By embracing God's design for fatherhood, you will not only raise godly children but also fulfill your divine calling with purpose and joy.

Chapter 2

The Heart of Discipline

What Is Biblical Discipline?

Discipline is often misunderstood as mere punishment or correction. However, in the biblical context, discipline is much deeper—it is a form of love, guidance, and training that shapes a child's heart and character. Biblical discipline is not about control, fear, or dominance but about teaching, nurturing, and leading children toward godly wisdom and maturity.

1. Biblical Discipline Is Rooted in Love

The foundation of biblical discipline is love. **Proverbs 3:11-12** says, *"My son, do not despise the Lord's discipline, and do not resent His rebuke, because the Lord disciplines those He loves, as a father the son he delights in."*

God's discipline is an expression of His love, not His anger. Likewise, a father's discipline should not stem from frustration or impatience but from a deep love and desire to see his children grow in wisdom and righteousness.

When a father disciplines his children in love, he:

- **Corrects with patience and understanding** rather than anger.
- **Guides rather than punishes**—the goal is transformation, not retribution.
- **Encourages a heart change** rather than just enforcing rules.

A father who disciplines in love teaches his children that correction is not rejection but an act of care.

2. Biblical Discipline Is Training, Not Just Punishment

Many parents equate discipline with punishment, but biblical discipline is about training, teaching, and guiding. **Proverbs 22:6** states, *"Train up a child in the way he should go, and when he is old, he will not depart from it."*

Training a child means shaping their heart and mind over time through:

- **Consistent teaching of God's Word.**
- **Setting clear expectations and boundaries.**

- Correcting behavior while reinforcing love and grace.

Punishment alone may temporarily stop bad behavior, but **training equips children to make godly choices even when their father is not around.**

3. Biblical Discipline Aims at the Heart, Not Just Behavior

True discipline goes beyond controlling actions; it seeks to transform the heart. **Matthew 15:18-19** says, *"But the things that come out of a person's mouth come from the heart, and these defile them."*

If a father only disciplines external behavior—like bad language, disobedience, or dishonesty—without addressing the **heart issues** behind those actions, real change will not happen. A godly father must go beyond "stop doing that" to **asking why the behavior is happening and addressing the root cause.**

For example:

- If a child lies, instead of just punishing them, a father should teach them the value of truthfulness.

- If a child is disrespectful, rather than just demanding respect, a father should help them understand humility and honor.

4. Biblical Discipline Is Consistent and Firm

God is unchanging in His discipline. **Hebrews 12:10-11** tells us, *"God disciplines us for our good, in order that we may share in His holiness. No discipline seems pleasant at the time, but painful. Later on, however, it produces a harvest of righteousness and peace for those who have been trained by it."*

A godly father must be **consistent** in discipline. Children should understand that consequences are not based on a father's mood but on clear, consistent expectations. If discipline is inconsistent, children become confused and may manipulate situations.

Consistency includes:

- **Following through on consequences.** If a child disobeys, the consequence should be enforced as previously stated.
- **Avoiding favoritism.** Discipline should be the same for all children.
- **Correcting with fairness.** Discipline should not be extreme or unreasonable.

A father who is firm but fair earns his children's respect and teaches them accountability.

5. Biblical Discipline Leads to Wisdom and Maturity

The purpose of discipline is to help children grow in wisdom and maturity. **Proverbs 29:15** says, *"The rod of correction imparts wisdom, but a child left undisciplined disgraces its mother."*

Discipline helps children learn:

- **Self-control** – They understand boundaries and learn to regulate their emotions.
- **Obedience to God** – They see discipline as part of spiritual growth.
- **Respect for authority** – They develop an attitude of humility and submission.
- **Wisdom in decision-making** – They grow in understanding right from wrong.

When fathers discipline their children biblically, they are preparing them to be responsible, godly adults who can lead their own families with wisdom.

Biblical discipline is not about power, control, or punishment—it is about **love, training, and guidance**. A godly father disciplines his children **not to break their**

spirit, but to shape their character. By disciplining with love, consistency, and a focus on the heart, a father fulfills his God-given role in raising children who walk in wisdom and righteousness.

As a father, you are not merely enforcing rules—you are **shaping a future generation.** Let your discipline be rooted in the principles of God's Word so that your children grow in wisdom, maturity, and godliness.

The Difference Between Discipline and Punishment

One of the biggest misconceptions about parenting is the idea that discipline and punishment are the same. While they may seem similar in practice, they have fundamentally different purposes and outcomes. A godly father must understand the difference between these two concepts to guide his children in a way that reflects God's love and wisdom.

1. Discipline vs. Punishment: Understanding the Difference

Aspect	Discipline	Punishment
Purpose	To teach and correct behavior for future growth	To penalize for past mistakes
Focus	The child's heart and character	The child's wrong action
Method	Instruction, guidance, and appropriate consequences	Often involves fear, shame, or harsh penalties
Outcome	Growth, wisdom, and improved decision-making	Fear, resentment, and potential rebellion
Biblical Model	Reflects God's loving correction (Hebrews 12:6)	Can reflect human anger rather than godly correction

Discipline is forward-focused—it aims to teach a child **how to make better choices** in the future. Punishment, on the other hand, often looks backward and simply penalizes without providing a learning experience.

For example, if a child disrespects a parent, punishment might involve immediate consequences without explanation. Discipline, however, would include:

1. **Correcting the behavior** (e.g., requiring an apology).
2. **Explaining why respect is important** (using biblical principles like *Ephesians 6:1-3*, which instructs children to honor their parents).
3. **Providing a clear expectation for future behavior** (reinforcing the importance of kindness and respect).

A father who disciplines instead of merely punishing helps his child develop **wisdom, self-control, and moral integrity**.

2. Biblical Examples of Discipline vs. Punishment

The Bible offers powerful examples of how discipline differs from punishment:

- **God's discipline of Israel (Deuteronomy 8:5)**: *"Know then in your heart that as a man disciplines his son, so the Lord your God disciplines you."* Even when Israel sinned, God corrected them to bring them back to righteousness.

- **The Prodigal Son (Luke 15:11-32)**: Instead of punishing his son harshly for wasting his inheritance, the father in the parable welcomed him back with love, using the experience as a lesson in grace and repentance.
- **David and Bathsheba (2 Samuel 12:1-14)**: After David sinned, God sent Nathan the prophet to **correct and discipline** him rather than simply punishing him. David repented and was restored.

A godly father must strive to **mirror God's discipline**, focusing on **correction, restoration, and teaching**, rather than punishment that stems from anger or frustration.

3. Correcting with Grace

Discipline should never be **about humiliation or breaking a child's spirit**. **Ephesians 6:4** warns, *"Fathers, do not exasperate your children; instead, bring them up in the training and instruction of the Lord."*

This means that discipline should:

- **Encourage repentance, not resentment.** A child should understand that correction is meant to help them, not hurt them.

- **Be proportional.** A punishment that far outweighs the mistake can lead to bitterness rather than learning.
- **Leave room for grace.** Just as God forgives us, children should experience both justice and mercy in discipline.

A father who understands this difference **builds trust** with his children rather than creating a relationship based on fear.

Teaching with Love, Not Fear

A godly father's discipline should always be **rooted in love**, not **motivated by fear, control, or frustration**. The way a father disciplines his children shapes their view of God, authority, and relationships.

1. The Dangers of Fear-Based Parenting

Some fathers believe that instilling fear is necessary to gain obedience, but this approach can have **negative long-term effects**:

- **Fear breeds secrecy.** A child afraid of punishment may choose to hide mistakes rather than seek guidance.

- **Fear damages relationships.** When children fear their father rather than respect him, they may withdraw emotionally.
- **Fear distorts their view of God.** If a child only experiences harsh punishment, they may grow up seeing God as a harsh judge rather than a loving Father.

The Bible reminds us in **1 John 4:18**, *"There is no fear in love. But perfect love drives out fear, because fear has to do with punishment."* A father should aim to **correct and teach with love**, not intimidation.

2. How to Teach with Love

Teaching with love does not mean avoiding discipline—it means disciplining in a way that **nurtures rather than wounds**. Here are ways a godly father can discipline with love:

- **Set clear expectations** – Children need to know the rules and consequences beforehand. This prevents them from feeling unfairly treated.
- **Stay calm during correction** – Proverbs 15:1 says, *"A gentle answer turns away wrath, but a harsh word stirs up anger."* A father who corrects with **patience and wisdom** is more effective than one who reacts in anger.

- **Explain the reason for discipline** – Children need to understand **why** they are being corrected. This helps them make better choices in the future.
- **Balance discipline with encouragement** – Just as a father corrects, he must also uplift. **Colossians 3:21** warns, *"Fathers, do not embitter your children, or they will become discouraged."*

3. Encouragement and Affirmation in Discipline

A godly father ensures that **discipline is not just about correction, but also about affirmation and encouragement**. After correcting a child, a father should:

- **Reassure them of his love.** Remind them that discipline is done **for their good**, not out of anger.
- **Affirm their value and potential.** Encourage them to make better choices rather than making them feel like a failure.
- **Pray with them.** Teaching children to bring their struggles to God fosters spiritual growth.

For example, if a child lies, after correction, the father can say:
"I love you, and I know you are an honest and strong person. I want you to grow into someone people can

trust. Let's pray together and ask God to help you always tell the truth."

This approach ensures that discipline leads to **growth, healing, and stronger relationships** rather than fear and shame.

Final Thoughts

A godly father disciplines **not to break his child's spirit, but to shape their heart**. He understands that:

- **Discipline is different from punishment.** It is about training for the future, not just penalizing the past.
- **Correction must be done with grace.** Children should feel loved, even in correction.
- **Teaching should be based on love, not fear.** Fear-based parenting leads to secrecy and resentment, but love-based discipline builds trust and wisdom.

By following the biblical model of discipline, a father **reflects God's heart** and raises children who are **wise, strong, and deeply rooted in faith**.

Chapter 3

Training Up a Child in the Way of the Lord

The role of a godly father goes beyond providing for his children's physical needs; he is responsible for their **spiritual growth** and **moral development**. Proverbs 22:6 instructs, *"Train up a child in the way he should go, and when he is old he will not depart from it."* This verse is not just advice—it is a divine principle that every Christian father should take seriously.

A father's guidance, prayers, and teachings have the power to shape his children into **faithful, God-fearing individuals** who will stand firm even when the world challenges their beliefs. This chapter will explore how a father can effectively instill Christian values from an early age, ensuring his children grow up with a strong spiritual foundation.

Instilling Christian Values from an Early Age

The values children learn in their formative years shape the kind of adults they will become. A father must be intentional in **imparting biblical principles**, ensuring that his children not only hear the Word of God but also see it lived out daily.

1. The Importance of Early Spiritual Training

Children are like **spiritual sponges**—they absorb everything they see and hear. By introducing **Christian values early**, a father lays a solid foundation that will guide his children throughout life.

- **Deuteronomy 6:6-7** emphasizes this responsibility:
  "These commandments that I give you today are to be on your hearts. Impress them on your children. Talk about them when you sit at home and when you walk along the road, when you lie down and when you get up."
- Studies have shown that **children develop their core values** by the time they are ten years old. What they learn in their early years significantly impacts their beliefs, behaviors, and decisions as they grow.

A godly father must **seize every opportunity** to plant the seeds of faith in his children's hearts.

---

2. Ways to Instill Christian Values

There are several practical ways a father can instill biblical values in his children:

A. Leading by Example

Children learn more from **what they see** than what they are told. A father who models **integrity, kindness, faithfulness, and love** teaches his children far more than just words ever could.

- **Be consistent in faith** – Pray, read the Bible, and serve God daily.
- **Demonstrate love and patience** – Treat others with kindness, especially within the family.
- **Practice honesty and integrity** – Never compromise godly principles for convenience.

1 Corinthians 11:1 reminds us, *"Follow my example, as I follow the example of Christ."* A father's life should reflect Christ so that his children will be inspired to walk in righteousness.

B. Establishing a Habit of Family Devotions

Regular **family devotions** are essential for spiritual growth. A father should create a **structured but enjoyable** time of worship, prayer, and Bible study with his children.

Practical Tips for Family Devotions:

- **Keep it simple but meaningful.** Choose short Bible stories, discuss their meaning, and encourage participation.
- **Make it interactive.** Allow children to ask questions, share their thoughts, and even lead prayers.
- **Be consistent.** Set a specific time daily or weekly for devotions.

By making **God's Word a central part of family life**, children will develop a deep love and understanding of Scripture.

C. Teaching Through Everyday Conversations

Faith should not be limited to Sundays or special occasions; it should be **woven into daily life**.

- **Use teachable moments.** When faced with situations—whether a sibling dispute, a school

challenge, or an act of kindness—connect them to biblical lessons.
- **Talk about God's presence.** Remind children that God is always with them, guiding and protecting them.
- **Encourage gratitude.** Teach them to thank God daily for His blessings, both big and small.

When a father **intentionally integrates faith into everyday conversations**, his children naturally grow to see **God's hand in all aspects of life**.

D. Encouraging a Heart of Worship

A father should **nurture a love for worship** in his children. This can include:

- **Teaching them Christian songs** from a young age.
- **Encouraging participation in church activities** (youth group, choir, Bible clubs).
- **Making worship joyful and exciting** so they develop a passion for honoring God.

Psalm 95:1 says, *"Come, let us sing for joy to the Lord; let us shout aloud to the Rock of our salvation."* Children who grow up loving worship will carry that passion into adulthood.

E. Teaching the Importance of Prayer

A child who learns to pray at a young age **develops a strong spiritual foundation**. A father should:

- **Pray with his children daily** (morning, meals, bedtime).
- **Encourage them to pray for others** (friends, family, teachers).
- **Teach them that prayer is a conversation with God, not just a ritual.**

Philippians 4:6 reminds us, *"Do not be anxious about anything, but in every situation, by prayer and petition, with thanksgiving, present your requests to God."* A father who prioritizes prayer raises children who trust in God's power.

F. Teaching Generosity and Service

Christian values include **helping others, sharing, and showing kindness**. A father should teach his children:

- **The joy of giving** – Encourage them to share with those in need.
- **The importance of service** – Involve them in church or community outreach.

- **Compassion and empathy** – Teach them to love others as Christ loves them.

Jesus said in **Acts 20:35**, *"It is more blessed to give than to receive."* Children who grow up with a giving heart **develop strong character and a deep love for others**.

---

3. The Long-Term Impact of Early Spiritual Training

When a father **consistently instills biblical values**, his children will:

■ **Develop strong moral character** – They will learn honesty, kindness, and responsibility.

■ **Make wise choices** – Biblical principles will guide their decisions.

■ **Stand firm in their faith** – They will be spiritually equipped to handle challenges.

■ **Carry their faith into the next generation** – They will pass on godly values to their own children.

Proverbs 20:7 states, *"The righteous who walks in his integrity—blessed are his children after him!"* A godly father's influence lasts beyond his lifetime.

Final Thoughts

Training a child in the way of the Lord requires **intentional effort, consistency, and prayer**. A father must:

✔ **Lead by example** – Live out the values he teaches.
✔ **Create a godly home environment** – Make faith an everyday priority.
✔ **Be patient and persistent** – Spiritual growth takes time.
✔ **Trust in God's promises** – Believe that the seeds sown today will bear fruit in the future.

By instilling Christian values from an early age, a father fulfills his **God-given role** in shaping the next generation **for Christ**. His children will grow up with a strong foundation of faith, wisdom, and godliness—ready to live a life that honors God.

A godly father's responsibility extends beyond material provision and discipline; he is called to shape his children's hearts and minds toward righteousness. This requires daily **spiritual nourishment** through devotions and prayer, as well as **intentional character-building** that instills integrity.

The world presents countless distractions and temptations that can lead children away from godly values. However, a father who prioritizes **daily spiritual discipline and character training** equips his children to stand firm in their faith and make wise, God-honoring decisions.

The Power of Daily Devotions and Prayer

One of the most powerful ways a father can influence his children's faith is by leading them in **daily devotions and prayer**. This consistent practice helps children:
■ **Develop a personal relationship with God**
■ **Understand biblical principles**
■ **Find strength in God's Word during challenges**
■ **Cultivate a lifestyle of gratitude and dependence on God**

1. The Role of a Father in Family Devotions

Fathers are called to be **spiritual leaders** in the home. Just as a shepherd guides his flock, a father must **lead his family in seeking God daily**. Deuteronomy 11:18-19 emphasizes this responsibility:

"Fix these words of mine in your hearts and minds; tie them as symbols on your hands and bind them on your foreheads. Teach them to your children, talking about

them when you sit at home and when you walk along the road, when you lie down and when you get up."

This passage highlights the **continuous nature** of teaching God's Word—it should be an integral part of everyday life, not just something reserved for Sundays.

2. Practical Ways to Incorporate Daily Devotions

A father doesn't need to be a Bible scholar to lead his family in devotions. What matters is **consistency, sincerity, and engagement**.

A. Set a Regular Time for Devotions

- Choose a time that works best for the family—morning, before bedtime, or during meals.
- Keep it **short and engaging**, especially for younger children.

B. Read Scripture Together

- Start with simple Bible stories and build up to deeper discussions.
- Use a **children's Bible** for younger kids and gradually introduce more complex passages.
- Encourage children to **ask questions and share insights**.

C. Apply the Bible to Daily Life

- Relate biblical principles to real-life situations.
- For example, if a child struggles with honesty, discuss **Proverbs 12:22** (*"The Lord detests lying lips, but he delights in people who are trustworthy."*).

D. Encourage Scripture Memorization

- Choose **one verse per week** and make it a fun challenge.
- Reward children when they successfully memorize and recite the verse.

3. Teaching Children the Habit of Prayer

Prayer is not just a **religious ritual**; it is a **personal conversation with God**. Teaching children to pray builds their **faith, confidence, and spiritual resilience**.

A. Teach Simple, Honest Prayers
Children don't need complicated words; they just need sincerity. Guide them to:

- Thank God for their blessings.
- Pray for family, friends, and those in need.
- Ask for wisdom, protection, and strength.

B. Model a Prayerful Life

A father should let his children see him **praying regularly**—both in private and in family settings. This teaches them that prayer is an essential part of daily life.

C. Encourage Personal Prayer Time

As children grow, they should develop their own **habit of private prayer**. A father can support this by:

- Giving them a personal prayer journal.
- Encouraging them to pray before making decisions.
- Reminding them that God is always listening.

By fostering **daily devotions and a strong prayer life**, a father nurtures **spiritually mature children** who will rely on God in every aspect of their lives.

Raising Children with Integrity and Character

Christian fatherhood is not just about **teaching religious principles**—it's about shaping children into **honest, responsible, and compassionate individuals** who reflect Christ in their daily lives. A father must **model**

and instill integrity, helping his children develop a strong moral compass.

1. What is Integrity?

Integrity means being **honest, trustworthy, and consistent in doing what is right**—even when no one is watching. It is about:
- Speaking the truth and keeping promises
- Doing the right thing, even when it's hard
- Standing firm in moral and biblical values

Proverbs 20:7 says, *"The righteous man walks in his integrity; his children are blessed after him."* A father who **lives with integrity** passes down a **legacy of righteousness** to his children.

2. How a Father Teaches Integrity

A father teaches integrity in two main ways:

1. **By example** – Children learn by watching. If a father **demonstrates honesty, fairness, and faithfulness**, his children will follow his lead.
2. **Through instruction** – A father must **explain the importance of integrity**, using biblical teachings and everyday situations to reinforce the lesson.

A. Modeling Integrity in Daily Life

A godly father must:

- **Be truthful** – Avoid lying or bending the truth, even in small matters.
- **Keep commitments** – Show children that a man's word should be trustworthy.
- **Admit mistakes and seek forgiveness** – Teach children that making mistakes is human, but honesty and repentance matter.
- **Treat others with fairness and respect** – Show kindness in business, friendships, and family relationships.

Example:
If a cashier accidentally gives too much change, a father should return it. This **teaches children honesty in action**, not just words.

B. Encouraging Honesty in Children

Integrity must be **reinforced in daily interactions**. Fathers should:

- **Praise honesty, even when the truth is hard to admit.**
- **Correct dishonesty gently but firmly.** Teach children that lying damages trust.
- **Tell Bible stories about integrity.** For example, the story of **Daniel refusing to compromise his**

faith (Daniel 6) is a powerful lesson on standing firm in righteousness.

C. Teaching Responsibility and Work Ethic

A child with integrity **takes responsibility for their actions and commitments**. A father should:

- **Assign age-appropriate chores** to develop a sense of duty.
- **Encourage follow-through on tasks** (e.g., finishing homework, completing responsibilities).
- **Teach that actions have consequences**—good or bad.

Proverbs 10:9 states, *"Whoever walks in integrity walks securely, but he who makes his ways crooked will be found out."* A child who learns responsibility will grow into a **trustworthy and disciplined adult**.

D. Teaching Compassion and Fairness

A godly father should cultivate **kindness, generosity, and a sense of justice** in his children. This can be done by:

- **Encouraging acts of kindness** (helping neighbors, giving to the needy).

- **Teaching them to stand up for what is right** (defending the weak, rejecting bullying).
- **Helping them develop empathy**—reminding them to consider others' feelings and perspectives.

Micah 6:8 sums it up beautifully: *"He has shown you, O man, what is good; and what does the Lord require of you but to do justly, to love mercy, and to walk humbly with your God?"*

Final Thoughts

Raising children in **daily devotion, prayer, and integrity** creates a **foundation of faith and character** that will last a lifetime. A godly father must:
✔ **Prioritize spiritual training through devotions and prayer.**
✔ **Model and teach integrity in all aspects of life.**
✔ **Instill responsibility, kindness, and fairness.**

By doing so, he fulfills God's calling to **train up a child in the way of the Lord**, leaving a legacy of **righteousness, faith, and godliness** for generations to come.

Chapter 4

Leading with Love and Authority

Raising children is a profound responsibility that requires a father to exercise both **love and authority**. A godly father is neither overly harsh nor overly permissive—he understands that parenting requires a delicate balance of **grace and discipline**.

Some fathers lean too heavily on authority, enforcing strict rules without fostering emotional connection. Others focus too much on grace, avoiding necessary correction to prevent conflict. However, Scripture teaches that **both love and discipline are necessary for raising godly children.**

Proverbs 3:11-12 reminds us:

"My son, do not despise the Lord's discipline, and do not resent his rebuke, because the Lord disciplines those he loves, as a father the son he delights in."

This verse reveals a **fundamental truth: Discipline is an act of love.** When properly applied, discipline does not push children away—it **guides them toward righteousness** and prepares them for a life of wisdom and godliness.

The Balance Between Grace and Discipline

A father's role is not just to **correct misbehavior** but also to **nurture his children's hearts**. When discipline is detached from grace, it leads to **fear and resentment**. When grace is detached from discipline, it leads to **entitlement and rebellion**. A wise father blends **firm correction with unconditional love**, just as God does with His children.

1. Understanding Grace in Parenting

Grace is **unmerited favor**—it is **love that is freely given, not based on performance**. When fathers show grace to their children, they:

- Provide **unconditional love**, even when children fail.
- Offer **forgiveness** and second chances.
- Recognize **children's struggles and weaknesses** with patience.
- Encourage **growth through guidance**, rather than just punishment.

A. The Example of God's Grace

God, our Heavenly Father, constantly extends grace to His children. The **parable of the prodigal son** (Luke 15:11-32) illustrates this perfectly. When the rebellious son returns home, his father does not reject him—he runs to embrace him. This **does not mean there were no consequences**, but it shows that **grace is always available**.

A godly father should reflect this **grace-filled approach**:

- When a child makes a mistake, a father should **listen and correct with kindness**.
- Instead of reacting in anger, he should **teach lessons that build character**.
- He should **make sure his child knows that love is not dependent on performance**.

B. Practical Ways to Show Grace

1. **Listen before reacting** – Give children a chance to explain before jumping to conclusions.
2. **Forgive freely** – Holding grudges against children creates a tense home environment.
3. **Encourage rather than shame** – Correct with wisdom, not humiliation.
4. **Extend second chances** – Allow children to learn from their mistakes and try again.

2. The Importance of Discipline in Parenting

While grace is essential, **discipline is equally crucial** in shaping a child's character. The Bible is clear that **without discipline, children are left vulnerable to foolishness and destruction**.

Proverbs 22:15 says:
"Folly is bound up in the heart of a child, but the rod of discipline will drive it far away."

Children do not naturally develop **self-control, wisdom, or respect for authority**—these qualities must be cultivated through loving correction.

A. Biblical Discipline Is About Teaching, Not Punishing

Many people confuse **discipline with punishment**, but they are not the same. **Punishment focuses on consequences**, while **discipline focuses on correction and growth**. A godly father disciplines to **build character, not to break the spirit**.

Hebrews 12:11 states:
"No discipline seems pleasant at the time, but painful. Later on, however, it produces a harvest of righteousness and peace for those who have been trained by it."

A father who disciplines in **love and wisdom** helps his children grow into **responsible, respectful, and spiritually mature adults**.

B. Practical Ways to Discipline with Love

1. **Be consistent** – Children need clear expectations and consistent consequences.
2. **Explain the 'why'** – Instead of just saying "Because I said so," help children understand the reason behind rules.
3. **Correct in private** – Public humiliation can damage a child's confidence and trust.
4. **Use logical consequences** – Instead of reacting in anger, ensure that the consequence matches the misbehavior (e.g., if a child refuses to clean up their toys, they lose the privilege of playing with them).
5. **Follow discipline with encouragement** – Let children know that discipline is about **helping them grow**, not punishing them for failure.

---

3. Finding the Right Balance

A godly father **never uses discipline as a weapon** to control his children. Instead, he **corrects with wisdom and love, always pointing them back to Christ**. The perfect example of this balance is seen in **Jesus' interactions with His disciples**.

A. Jesus' Example of Leading with Love and Authority
Jesus was **both gentle and firm**:
✔ He **corrected His disciples when they lacked faith** (Matthew 8:26).
✔ He **rebuked Peter when he spoke foolishly** (Matthew 16:23).
✔ Yet, He **showed incredible patience and love** toward them.

This is the **model for godly fatherhood**—firm, yet full of compassion.

B. Practical Steps to Maintain Balance

1. **Pray for wisdom daily** – Ask God to help you navigate discipline and grace wisely.
2. **Set clear expectations** – When children know what is expected, they are less likely to push boundaries.
3. **Be emotionally present** – Children respond best to discipline when they feel genuinely loved.

4. **Apologize when needed** – If a father disciplines out of anger or harshness, he should model humility by asking for forgiveness.

Colossians 3:21 warns:
"Fathers, do not embitter your children, or they will become discouraged."

A father who is **overly harsh** risks pushing his children away, while a father who is **too lenient** fails to prepare them for real-world responsibilities. The **goal is to guide them in truth, while surrounding them with love.**

Fatherhood is **a sacred calling** that requires **both authority and grace**. A godly father must:
✔ **Demonstrate unconditional love and patience.**
✔ **Discipline wisely, focusing on correction rather than punishment.**
✔ **Lead by example, modeling both obedience to God and compassion.**
✔ **Trust in God's wisdom, seeking His guidance in every step of parenting.**

A father who **masters the balance between grace and discipline** raises children who are not only **obedient** but also **secure in their father's love**. More importantly, he

reflects the heart of God, teaching his children the beauty of following Christ in both truth and love.

A godly father's responsibility extends beyond discipline; it also involves **correcting with patience and wisdom** while consistently **encouraging and affirming** his children. Discipline that is detached from patience leads to frustration, and correction without encouragement can leave children feeling discouraged and inadequate. A father must always strive to balance these aspects, ensuring that his children grow into confident, godly individuals who understand their worth in Christ.

Correcting with Patience and Wisdom

The way a father **corrects his children** has a **lasting impact** on their emotional, spiritual, and mental well-being. Proverbs 15:1 teaches:

"A gentle answer turns away wrath, but a harsh word stirs up anger."

This verse reminds us that correction should be **gentle, not harsh**. A father who disciplines **out of frustration** may end up wounding his child's heart instead of guiding them toward wisdom. **Correction should be intentional, patient, and rooted in love.**

1. The Dangers of Harsh Discipline

Harsh discipline can result in:
- **Fear instead of respect** – Children may obey out of fear rather than understanding.
- **Resentment toward authority** – Overly strict discipline can lead children to rebel.
- **Low self-worth** – Constant criticism without patience can make children feel like they are never good enough.
- **Emotional distance** – A father who frequently yells or punishes harshly may push his children away emotionally.

Ephesians 6:4 warns:

"Fathers, do not provoke your children to anger, but bring them up in the discipline and instruction of the Lord."

A godly father must **avoid anger-driven correction** and instead guide his children with **patience and wisdom**.

2. How to Correct with Patience

■ **Stay Calm Before Correcting**

- If emotions are high, **pause and pray** before addressing misbehavior.
- A father should **never discipline in anger**.
- Take a moment to reflect: *Is this correction coming from love or frustration?*

Listen Before Reacting

- Give the child a chance to explain their side of the story.
- Proverbs 18:13 says, *"To answer before listening—that is folly and shame."*
- Understanding a child's motives helps a father correct with wisdom.

Use Logical and Fair Consequences

- Ensure that the discipline **matches the misbehavior** (e.g., taking away screen time for not completing chores).
- Avoid punishments that are **too severe or unrelated to the offense**.
- The goal is **teaching responsibility, not exerting power**.

Explain the Lesson Behind the Correction

- Instead of saying, *"Because I said so,"* a godly father explains *why* rules exist.

- Example: *"I'm disciplining you because I love you and want you to learn responsibility."*
- When children understand the reasoning, they are **more likely to accept correction with a willing heart.**

■ Reaffirm Love After Discipline

- Make sure children **know they are still loved** even after discipline.
- Example: *"I corrected you because I care about your future, but I will always love you no matter what."*
- Follow up discipline with **a hug, a kind word, or reassurance.**

A patient and wise father recognizes that **his role is not to break his child's spirit but to guide them in truth and righteousness.**

The Role of Encouragement and Affirmation

While discipline shapes a child's behavior, **encouragement and affirmation** shape their **confidence, faith, and self-worth.** Children need to

hear words of affirmation just as much as they need correction. A father who **only corrects but never affirms** may raise children who feel unloved, insecure, or discouraged.

Proverbs 16:24 says:

"Gracious words are a honeycomb, sweet to the soul and healing to the bones."

A father's **words carry immense power**—they can **build up** or **tear down** a child's heart.

1. The Power of Encouragement in Parenting

Encouragement helps children:
- **Develop confidence** – They believe in their abilities and self-worth.
- **Stay motivated** – Positive words push them to keep trying, even after failure.
- **Feel secure in their father's love** – They understand that love is not based on perfection.
- **Grow in faith** – Encouragement leads them to trust in God's plan for their life.

2. Ways to Encourage and Affirm Your Child

- **Speak Life with Your Words**

- Avoid negative words like *"You'll never get it right"* or *"Why can't you be more like your sibling?"*
- Instead, say:
    - *"I'm proud of you for trying your best."*
    - *"God has a great purpose for your life."*
    - *"You are growing into a strong and wise person."*

■ Recognize Their Strengths

- Every child has unique talents and abilities.
- Take time to say, *"I see the way you help others—you have a kind heart."*
- Help them develop their gifts by providing **opportunities to grow.**

■ Praise Effort, Not Just Achievement

- Instead of only praising success, affirm their effort.
- Example: *"I love how hard you worked on that project, even though it was difficult."*
- This teaches children that **persistence matters more than perfection**.

■ Pray Over Your Children

- Let them **hear you pray for them**, speaking words of **blessing and faith**.
- Example: *"Lord, bless my child and guide them in Your wisdom and love."*
- Praying over children helps them feel **secure in God's love**.

■ Be Present and Supportive

- Encouragement is not just about words—it's also about **being involved**.
- Attend their events, celebrate their wins, and comfort them during struggles.
- A father's **presence and support** are among the greatest affirmations a child can receive.

Final Thoughts

A godly father **balances correction with encouragement**, ensuring that his children grow in both **wisdom and confidence**.

✔ **Discipline should be patient, wise, and rooted in love.**
✔ **Correction should be fair, calm, and always followed by reassurance.**
✔ **Encouragement and affirmation help children develop strong self-worth and faith.**

✔ **A father's words and actions shape his child's heart, so he must be intentional in both.**

By leading with **love, wisdom, discipline, and encouragement**, a godly father reflects **the character of Christ**—a model of **both truth and grace.**

Chapter 5

Building Strong Family Relationships

Family relationships are the foundation of a child's emotional, spiritual, and psychological development. A godly father's role extends beyond providing discipline and instruction—he must also **nurture, guide, and support** his children through **consistent love and presence**. The strength of a family is built through intentional effort, where each member feels valued, heard, and supported.

In this chapter, we will explore one of the most **powerful yet often overlooked gifts a father can give his family—the gift of time.**

Being Present: The Gift of Time

One of the most **valuable investments** a father can make in his family is his **time**. In today's fast-paced world, many fathers are **physically present but emotionally**

absent due to work commitments, technology distractions, and other pressures. However, the most lasting impact on a child's life is not **money, gifts, or material possessions**—it is the **intentional presence** of a loving father.

Psalm 127:3 reminds us:

"Children are a heritage from the Lord, offspring a reward from Him."

Children are **a blessing**, and fathers are **entrusted by God** to nurture them with love and attention. **A father's presence—or absence—shapes a child's future.**

1. The Impact of a Father's Presence

When a father is **actively involved** in his children's lives, they experience:

■ **Greater Emotional Security**

- Children who feel their father is available and engaged develop **higher self-esteem** and emotional stability.
- They are less likely to struggle with anxiety, depression, or feelings of rejection.

■ Stronger Moral and Spiritual Foundation

- A present father instills **Christian values, faith, and integrity** in his children.
- Proverbs 22:6 says, *"Train up a child in the way he should go, and even when he is old, he will not depart from it."*

■ Better Behavior and Decision-Making

- Studies show that children with involved fathers are **less likely** to engage in destructive behavior, rebellion, or poor decision-making.
- A father's **guidance and support** help children develop **self-discipline and accountability**.

■ Stronger Family Bonds

- When a father spends **quality time** with his family, it creates **a deep emotional connection** that strengthens the home.
- **Memories built together** form the foundation of a child's lifelong relationship with their father.

On the other hand, when a father is **physically absent or emotionally distant**, children may experience:

🚫 **Low self-worth** – Feeling unloved or unimportant.
🚫 **Difficulty forming healthy relationships** – Struggles with trust, communication, and emotional

connection.

🚫 **Increased risk of rebellion** – Seeking validation outside the home, often in unhealthy ways.

🚫 **Spiritual disconnection** – Without a strong role model, faith can feel irrelevant or distant.

God calls fathers to **be present, engaged, and intentional** in building **strong family relationships**.

---

2. Practical Ways to Be Present as a Father

Being present does **not** mean simply being in the same room. True presence involves **intentional engagement, listening, and participating** in family life.

Here are some **practical ways** a godly father can **give the gift of time** to his family:

A. Prioritize Family Time

- Set aside **dedicated time** for your family each day.
- Avoid **bringing work home** or letting distractions take away from **family moments**.
- **Example:** Have dinner together and use the time to talk about the day.

B. Engage in Meaningful Conversations

- Ask open-ended questions like, *"How was your day?"* or *"What's something new you learned today?"*
- Actively **listen** to your children's concerns, fears, and joys.
- Avoid distractions like your phone while your child is speaking.

C. Create Special Family Traditions

- Traditions build **lifelong memories** and strengthen **family identity**.
- Some ideas include:
  - ■ **Weekly family devotionals** – Study the Bible together.
  - ■ **Father-child outings** – One-on-one time with each child.
  - ■ **Game nights, storytelling, or outdoor activities** – Bond through fun experiences.

D. Be Involved in Their Interests

- Show interest in **what your children love**—sports, hobbies, music, or school activities.

- Attend their **school events, games, or performances** to support their efforts.
- A child feels valued when they see their father **celebrating their achievements**.

E. Lead by Example

- **Show Christ-like love** by **being kind, patient, and forgiving** in your home.
- Demonstrate **the values you teach**—prayer, integrity, hard work, and respect.
- Children learn more from **what they see in their father's actions** than from words alone.

F. Put Away Distractions

- **Technology should not replace connection**—avoid being glued to the TV or phone when spending time with family.
- Set aside **device-free zones**, such as during meals or bedtime conversations.
- **Being mentally and emotionally available** is just as important as being physically present.

G. Pray with and for Your Family

- One of the most **powerful ways to lead as a father** is through **prayer**.

- Pray for your children's **spiritual growth, future, and daily struggles**.
- Let them **hear you pray over them**, reinforcing that God is their ultimate Father and protector.

A father's **presence** in his children's lives is **one of the greatest gifts** he can offer. **No amount of money or success can replace the love, time, and attention** a father gives to his family.

✔ **A godly father prioritizes time with his family over distractions.**
✔ **He understands that his children's hearts are shaped by his presence and guidance.**
✔ **He listens, engages, and builds a legacy of love, faith, and integrity.**
✔ **By being present, he reflects God's love—the ultimate Father who is always near His children.**

Psalm 103:13 reminds us:

"As a father has compassion on his children, so the Lord has compassion on those who fear Him."

Fathers who **invest time, love, and presence** into their families leave behind **a legacy that lasts for generations**.

In the previous section, we explored the **importance of a father's presence** in his children's lives and how quality time strengthens family bonds. However, building a strong, godly family goes beyond just spending time together—it requires **intentionally creating a Christ-centered home** and **fostering open communication** within the family.

A godly father understands that his home is more than just a place where his family sleeps and eats—it is a **spiritual sanctuary** where faith is nurtured, love is displayed, and biblical values are instilled.

In this section, we will examine how a father can **lead his household in Christ** and build a family culture rooted in **faith, love, and communication.**

Creating a Christ-Centered Home

A Christ-centered home is one where **Jesus is at the heart of everything**—the family's decisions, conversations, values, and daily routines. As the spiritual leader of the home, a father has a **divine responsibility** to guide his family toward **knowing and honoring God.**

1. The Role of a Father in Leading His Home Spiritually

Scripture calls fathers to **shepherd their families** in faith. Ephesians 6:4 states:

"Fathers, do not provoke your children to anger, but bring them up in the discipline and instruction of the Lord."

A godly father:

■ **Prioritizes faith in the home** – Everything in the household should reflect God's truth and love.
■ **Teaches his children about God** – He actively **shares biblical lessons** and ensures his family understands God's Word.
■ **Sets a spiritual example** – His actions should **mirror the teachings of Christ** so that his children follow his lead.

A father should not **outsource spiritual training** to the church alone—it begins **at home** with his **daily example** and involvement.

---

2. Practical Ways to Create a Christ-Centered Home

Building a faith-filled home requires **daily intentional efforts**. Here are ways a father can **cultivate a spiritual atmosphere** in his home:

A. Establish Family Worship and Devotions

- **Daily or weekly family devotions** keep God's Word at the center of family life.
- **Read the Bible together**, discuss Scripture, and pray as a family.
- Create **a devotional routine** (e.g., before school, after dinner, or at bedtime).

Example: A father can read a short Bible passage and ask his children questions like:

- *"What do you think this verse means?"*
- *"How can we apply this to our lives today?"*

This simple practice **strengthens faith and encourages spiritual discussions** within the home.

B. Lead in Prayer and Teach Your Children to Pray

- **Pray over your children daily**—for their **protection, wisdom, and faith**.
- Encourage them to pray before meals, at bedtime, and in times of difficulty.

- Teach them **that prayer is a conversation with God**, not just a ritual.

"The prayer of a righteous person is powerful and effective." (James 5:16)

When children **see their father praying**, they learn that faith is not just words—it is **a relationship with God**.

C. Foster a Culture of Worship

- Fill your home with **worship music** and **songs of praise**.
- Encourage **joyful worship**, teaching your children that loving God is not just about rules, but also about **celebration and gratitude**.
- Attend **church together as a family**, emphasizing that worship is a priority.

Example: A father can **turn car rides into worship time** by playing Christian music and singing along with his children.

D. Encourage Scripture Memorization

Psalm 119:11 says: *"I have hidden Your word in my heart that I might not sin against You."*

- Challenge your children to **memorize Bible verses** and discuss their meanings.
- Create **fun memory games** to help them recall Scripture.
- **Use visual reminders**—place Bible verses around the house (on walls, mirrors, or the refrigerator).

When children **internalize God's Word**, it **shapes their thoughts and decisions** as they grow.

E. Live Out Biblical Values

A Christ-centered home must be filled with **love, grace, and godly values**.

- **Show kindness, patience, and forgiveness** in your interactions.
- **Model servant leadership** by putting your family's needs above your own.
- **Practice gratitude and contentment**, teaching your children to trust God's provision.

A father's actions speak louder than words. The way he **treats his wife, handles conflict, and prioritizes**

faith teaches his children more than any lesson he can preach.

The Importance of Open Communication

Another essential element of a strong family relationship is **open and honest communication**. Many families struggle with **poor communication**, which leads to misunderstandings, tension, and emotional distance.

A godly father must **create a safe environment** where his children feel **loved, heard, and understood**.

1. Why Open Communication Matters

Proverbs 18:13 says:

"To answer before listening—that is folly and shame."

A father should **listen before speaking** and create a culture where his children feel comfortable expressing themselves.

Open communication:

■ **Builds trust** – Children are more likely to seek guidance when they know they will be heard.
■ **Strengthens emotional connection** – Talking openly fosters deeper relationships.
■ **Prevents rebellion and secrecy** – When children feel unheard, they may withdraw or seek validation elsewhere.

2. Practical Ways to Improve Communication in the Home

A. Listen Without Judgment

- Give your children **your full attention** when they speak.
- Avoid dismissing their feelings or **immediately correcting them**—sometimes, they just need to be heard.
- Repeat what they say to **show understanding** (*"So what you're saying is..."*).

B. Have Regular Family Meetings

- Set aside time for **family discussions** about important matters.

- Allow each family member to **voice their thoughts and concerns**.
- Use this time to **pray together and encourage one another**.

Example: A father can host **a weekly "family check-in"** where everyone shares their highs and lows of the week.

C. Encourage Honesty

- Let your children know they can be **honest without fear of harsh punishment**.
- When they confess mistakes, **respond with grace and guidance** instead of anger.
- Create **a safe space** where they feel valued and respected.

D. Be Approachable and Available

- Be **emotionally available**, not just physically present.
- If your child wants to talk, **drop what you're doing and listen**.
- Show them they are a **priority** in your life.

E. Teach Conflict Resolution

- Teach your children how to **express disagreements respectfully**.
- Show them how to **apologize and forgive**.
- Guide them in solving problems **without anger or resentment**.

"A soft answer turns away wrath, but a harsh word stirs up anger." (Proverbs 15:1)

When a father models **healthy communication**, his children **learn how to handle relationships** with love and wisdom.

Final Thoughts

A godly father **builds his home on the foundation of Christ** and **strengthens his family through love and communication**.

✔ **A Christ-centered home reflects God's love in every aspect of family life.**

✔ Children thrive when they feel heard, valued, and spiritually guided.
✔ A father's presence, leadership, and open communication create a lasting legacy.

By prioritizing **faith, love, and connection**, a father **raises children who walk in God's ways** and build strong families for generations to come.

Chapter 6

Overcoming Challenges in Fatherhood

Fatherhood is one of the most rewarding yet challenging roles a man can have. As a father, you are not only a provider and protector but also a **mentor, guide, and spiritual leader** for your children. While the journey of fatherhood is filled with moments of joy and fulfillment, it also comes with its fair share of **difficulties—disobedience, rebellion, discipline issues, and personal struggles.**

Many fathers feel overwhelmed by these challenges and sometimes question whether they are doing enough. However, God's Word provides **wisdom and guidance** on how to **navigate fatherhood with strength, patience, and faith.**

One of the greatest struggles fathers face is **how to handle disobedience in a godly and effective way**. In this chapter, we will explore how a father can **address disobedience with wisdom, balance discipline with love, and lead his children toward righteousness.**

Handling Disobedience with Wisdom

Every child, no matter how well-raised, will test boundaries at some point. Disobedience is a natural part of childhood and adolescence, but how a father **responds to it** will determine whether his child learns from it or continues in rebellion.

As fathers, it is tempting to react **out of frustration or anger**, but Scripture reminds us that discipline should be handled with **wisdom, patience, and love**.

Proverbs 22:6 instructs:
"Train up a child in the way he should go; even when he is old, he will not depart from it."

This verse emphasizes that **guidance and correction are necessary** in raising children. But how can a father do this effectively?

1. Understanding the Root of Disobedience

Before disciplining a child, a wise father should first seek to **understand why the child is being disobedient**. Children misbehave for various reasons, including:

- **Seeking attention** – Some children act out when they feel ignored or neglected.
- **Testing boundaries** – Kids naturally push limits to see how far they can go.
- **Emotional struggles** – Anxiety, frustration, and fear can lead to defiance.
- **Influence from peers or media** – Friends, television, and social media can encourage disobedient behavior.
- **Lack of clear expectations** – If rules are inconsistent or unclear, children may struggle to obey.

Instead of **reacting immediately with punishment**, a father should take time to **observe, listen, and pray for discernment** about what is causing the behavior.

---

2. Responding with Patience and Self-Control

A father's response to disobedience should **reflect God's patience and grace**.

James 1:19 advises:
"Let every man be swift to hear, slow to speak, and slow to wrath."

When a child misbehaves, a father should:

■ **Stay calm** – Avoid yelling or reacting in anger. Take a deep breath before responding.
■ **Listen first** – Ask the child why they acted the way they did.
■ **Correct with clarity** – Clearly explain **what they did wrong** and why it is unacceptable.
■ **Avoid humiliation** – Discipline should **correct behavior**, not shame the child.
■ **Be consistent** – Enforce the same rules fairly, without favoritism or inconsistency.

When a child sees that their father **handles discipline with fairness and wisdom**, they will learn **respect, self-control, and responsibility.**

---

3. Establishing Clear Expectations and Consequences

A father must set **firm but loving boundaries** in the home.

Ephesians 6:4 reminds fathers:
"Fathers, do not provoke your children to anger, but bring them up in the discipline and instruction of the Lord."

How can fathers **set clear expectations**?

✔ **Define household rules** – Make sure your child knows what is expected of them.

✔ **Explain the "why" behind the rules** – Teach them that rules are meant for **their safety and growth**, not just control.

✔ **Use logical consequences** – The punishment should match the offense. For example:

- If a child **refuses to do homework**, they might lose screen time.
- If they **disrespect someone**, they should write an apology letter or make amends.

When children understand that **rules and consequences are fair and consistent**, they are more likely to respect them.

---

4. Correcting Behavior While Maintaining a Strong Relationship

Some fathers are either **too harsh or too lenient**. A godly father corrects **without crushing his child's spirit**.

Colossians 3:21 warns:
"Fathers, do not provoke your children, lest they become discouraged."

Balancing discipline and love means:

✔ **Affirming your child's worth even when correcting them** – Say things like, *"I love you, but this behavior is unacceptable."*
✔ **Avoiding excessive punishment** – Make sure discipline is **fair and appropriate**.
✔ **Restoring the relationship after correction** – After discipline, reassure them of your love.

---

5. Leading by Example

Children learn more from **what they see** than from what they hear. A father must **model the obedience, patience, and respect** he wants to see in his children.

If a father:
- **Loses his temper easily**, his children will struggle with self-control.
- **Lies or breaks promises**, his children will struggle with honesty.
- **Disrespects their mother**, his children will not learn how to honor authority.

Instead, a godly father should:
✔ Apologize when he makes mistakes.

✔ Show respect and kindness to his wife and others.
✔ Be honest, patient, and disciplined in his own life.

Children **imitate their parents**, so a father who **models godly behavior** teaches his children how to walk in righteousness.

Handling disobedience is a challenge that every father will face. However, with **wisdom, patience, and biblical guidance**, a father can **correct his children in love without breaking their spirit**.

A godly father:

■ **Understands the root of disobedience** before reacting.
■ **Responds with patience and wisdom**, rather than anger.
■ **Sets clear expectations and fair consequences**.
■ **Balances discipline with love**, ensuring his child feels valued.
■ **Leads by example**, demonstrating the behavior he expects.

When a father corrects with **love, wisdom, and consistency**, he **not only shapes his child's behavior** but also **guides their heart toward God**.

Proverbs 13:24 states:
"Whoever spares the rod hates their child, but the one who loves their child is careful to discipline them."

Discipline is not about punishment—it is about training children in the way of the Lord.

Being a godly father in today's world comes with **unique challenges**. Among them are the **influence of culture and media** and the struggle to **maintain faith during difficult times**. The world is constantly shaping children's values through social media, entertainment, and societal norms. A father must **stand firm in his role as a spiritual leader**, guiding his children to remain faithful to God despite these challenges.

Let's explore how fathers can **combat negative cultural influences** and **strengthen their family's faith through hardships**.

Dealing with the Influence of Culture and Media

We live in a digital age where **media, social trends, and secular values** have a profound impact on children. Many fathers struggle with how to **protect their**

children from ungodly influences while still allowing them to engage with the world responsibly.

Romans 12:2 reminds us:
"Do not be conformed to this world, but be transformed by the renewing of your mind, that you may prove what is that good and acceptable and perfect will of God."

As a father, your goal is to **help your children filter what they see, hear, and believe** so they can stand firm in their faith.

---

1. Being Aware of What Influences Your Children

Children are constantly absorbing messages from:
- Social media (TikTok, Instagram, YouTube, etc.)
- Movies, music, and video games
- Friends and peer pressure
- School and societal values

Some of these influences may align with biblical teachings, while others can **subtly erode Christian values**. A wise father takes time to **observe and understand what is shaping his child's beliefs**.

Practical Steps:
✔ **Monitor media consumption** – Be mindful of what they watch, listen to, and engage with.

✔ **Discuss cultural issues** – Have open conversations about topics like identity, morality, and biblical truth.
✔ **Teach critical thinking** – Help them discern **right from wrong** based on Scripture.
✔ **Encourage godly friendships** – Surround them with **positive role models and Christian peers.**

---

2. Setting Biblical Standards for Media and Entertainment

A father must set **boundaries** on what is allowed in the home. Instead of just saying **"No"** to worldly content, guide your children toward **wholesome, faith-building alternatives.**

Philippians 4:8 says:
"Whatever is true, whatever is noble, whatever is right, whatever is pure, whatever is lovely, whatever is admirable—if anything is excellent or praiseworthy—think about such things."

How to set godly media standards:
■ **Create a family media plan** – Set limits on screen time and approve content in advance.
■ **Model responsible media use** – Children follow your example. Avoid watching inappropriate content yourself.

■ **Promote Christian entertainment** – Encourage movies, books, and music that align with biblical values.
■ **Teach digital responsibility** – Talk about online safety, cyberbullying, and the importance of honoring God online.

When children see that **media choices reflect their faith**, they will develop a **strong moral foundation** that withstands cultural pressures.

---

3. Teaching Biblical Identity Over Cultural Identity

One of the greatest dangers of modern culture is that it tries to **redefine identity** based on trends rather than God's Word.

The world says:
✘ "Your worth is based on your looks, success, or popularity."
✘ "You can believe whatever feels right to you."
✘ "Right and wrong are relative."

But the Bible says:
■ "You are fearfully and wonderfully made." (Psalm 139:14)
■ "Jesus is the way, the truth, and the life." (John 14:6)

■ "God's Word is eternal and unchanging." (Isaiah 40:8)

A godly father helps his children **stand firm in biblical truth**, even when the world pressures them to compromise.

How to teach biblical identity:
✔ **Affirm their worth in Christ** – Constantly remind them that their identity is **rooted in God's love**.
✔ **Encourage them to seek wisdom in Scripture** – Teach them to turn to the Bible, not culture, for answers.
✔ **Pray for their spiritual protection** – Cover them in prayer, asking God to guard their hearts and minds.

Strengthening Faith During Difficult Times

Life is filled with **challenges—financial struggles, loss, illness, and disappointments**. Children will look to their father for guidance when facing hardships. A godly father must **demonstrate unwavering faith**, showing his family that **God remains faithful in all circumstances**.

Proverbs 3:5-6 says:
"Trust in the Lord with all your heart, and do not lean on your own understanding. In all your ways acknowledge Him, and He will direct your paths."

How can a father **keep his family's faith strong during trials?**

---

1. Being a Spiritual Anchor in the Home

A father is called to be the **spiritual rock of his household**. When difficulties arise, he must lead with **faith, not fear**.

Ways to strengthen your family spiritually:
✔ **Pray together daily** – Make prayer a central part of your family's life.
✔ **Read and apply Scripture** – Turn to the Bible for guidance in times of trouble.
✔ **Be a source of encouragement** – Offer hope, reassurance, and biblical wisdom.
✔ **Demonstrate trust in God** – Show your children that faith remains strong, even in uncertainty.

When a father **remains steadfast in faith**, his family will learn to **lean on God** rather than panic in difficult moments.

2. Teaching Perseverance and God's Sovereignty

Many children struggle with **doubt and fear** during hard times. They may ask:
- *"Why did God let this happen?"*
- *"Does God really care about our problems?"*

A godly father teaches his children that:
- ■ **God is always in control** (Romans 8:28).
- ■ **Faith is strengthened through trials** (James 1:2-3).
- ■ **Hard times build character and trust in God** (Romans 5:3-5).

Encourage your children to:
- ✔ **Look for God's blessings** even in difficulties.
- ✔ **Pray for strength** rather than complaining.
- ✔ **Hold on to God's promises** found in Scripture.

3. Cultivating a Family Culture of Faith and Gratitude

A strong faith is built through **daily habits** of worship, gratitude, and trust in God.

How to make faith a lifestyle:
- ■ **Celebrate answered prayers** – Remind your family

of past victories.

■ **Speak faith-filled words** – Avoid negativity; instead, declare God's promises.

■ **Teach contentment** – Show your children how to be thankful, even in hard times.

■ **Remain joyful** – Joy is a testimony of faith that inspires children to trust in God.

A father who **leads his family with faith, love, and perseverance** leaves a **legacy of unwavering trust in God**.

Final Thoughts

A godly father **cannot shield his children from every challenge**, but he can **equip them with biblical wisdom** to navigate difficulties.

Key Takeaways:

■ **Cultural and media influences** shape children's values—parents must guide them wisely.

■ **Setting boundaries** for entertainment choices protects their faith.

■ **Biblical identity must be stronger than cultural identity.**

■ **During hard times, faith must be modeled through prayer, trust, and perseverance.**

■ A father's faith impacts the entire family—his example will shape generations.

As a father, **your role is not just to provide, but to lead your family spiritually**. By standing strong against cultural pressures and demonstrating **unshakable faith in trials**, you leave a **legacy of godliness that endures beyond your lifetime**.

Chapter 7

Teaching Responsibility and Hard Work

One of the most valuable lessons a father can teach his children is the **importance of responsibility and hard work**. In a world that often prioritizes convenience and shortcuts, instilling a **strong work ethic** in children is essential for their character, future success, and ability to serve God with diligence.

The Bible emphasizes the value of hard work and responsibility:

- **Proverbs 22:29** – *"Do you see someone skilled in their work? They will serve before kings; they will not serve before obscure men."*
- **Colossians 3:23** – *"Whatever you do, work at it with all your heart, as working for the Lord, not for human masters."*
- **Proverbs 6:6-8** – *"Go to the ant, you sluggard; consider its ways and be wise! It has no commander, no overseer or ruler, yet it stores its*

provisions in summer and gathers its food at harvest."

Teaching children **diligence, responsibility, and perseverance** will prepare them to succeed in life, contribute to society, and serve God faithfully. This chapter explores **practical ways fathers can instill a strong work ethic in their children** from an early age.

Instilling a Strong Work Ethic in Children

A **work ethic** is more than just teaching children to complete tasks—it's about developing a mindset of **discipline, perseverance, integrity, and responsibility**. Here's how fathers can instill these values in their children.

1. Teaching the Biblical Perspective on Work

Children should understand that work is not a punishment but a **God-given responsibility and privilege**. Many people view work as something to avoid, but Scripture teaches that:

■ **God worked first** – In Genesis, we see that **God worked** to create the world and rested afterward (Genesis 2:2).

■ **Work is a way to honor God** – Colossians 3:23 reminds us to work **wholeheartedly as for the Lord.**

■ **Diligence leads to success** – Proverbs 10:4 states, *"Lazy hands make for poverty, but diligent hands bring wealth."*

Children must learn that **work is not just about making money—it's about being responsible, disciplined, and honoring God in all they do.**

---

2. Setting the Example: Modeling a Strong Work Ethic

Children learn by watching their parents. If a father is **diligent, responsible, and hardworking**, his children will likely adopt the same habits.

- **Be diligent in your own work** – Show your children what commitment, discipline, and perseverance look like.
- **Demonstrate a positive attitude** – Avoid complaining about work. Instead, express gratitude for the ability to work.
- **Let them see your integrity** – Be honest and ethical

in your work, showing them that character matters more than shortcuts.

A father's **daily attitude toward work** will shape his children's perception of responsibility and effort.

---

3. Giving Age-Appropriate Responsibilities

Children develop a strong work ethic when they learn **to take responsibility** for their actions and contribute to the family.

How to assign responsibilities by age:
- **Toddlers (Ages 2-4):** Simple tasks like putting away toys, helping set the table, or carrying small items.
- **Young Children (Ages 5-8):** Making their bed, feeding pets, helping with dishes, and cleaning up after themselves.
- **Preteens (Ages 9-12):** Doing laundry, mowing the lawn, cooking simple meals, and completing homework independently.
- **Teenagers (Ages 13-18):** Managing their own schedules, budgeting their allowance, helping with major household chores, and possibly having a part-time job.

- **Be consistent** – Children should understand that work is a regular part of life, not something to avoid.

* **Praise their efforts** – Acknowledge their hard work and encourage them to take pride in their accomplishments.
* **Teach follow-through** – Ensure that children complete tasks they start and do them well.

When children learn **responsibility early**, they develop confidence, independence, and a sense of accomplishment.

---

4. Encouraging a Spirit of Excellence

A strong work ethic is not just about getting things done—it's about doing things **with excellence**. Teach children to:

■ **Give their best effort** – Whether it's schoolwork, chores, or sports, they should strive for excellence.
■ **Pay attention to details** – Teach them that small things matter and that quality work brings satisfaction.
■ **Take ownership of their work** – If they make mistakes, they should take responsibility, fix them, and learn from them.

Proverbs 16:3 says:
"Commit to the Lord whatever you do, and He will establish your plans."

By instilling a **commitment to excellence**, fathers prepare their children to be leaders in their future careers, ministries, and personal lives.

---

5. Teaching the Value of Perseverance

Hard work often involves **challenges and setbacks**. Children must learn that **failure is part of growth** and that perseverance leads to success.

How to teach perseverance:
✔ **Encourage them to finish what they start** – Whether it's a school project, a chore, or a hobby, they must see things through.
✔ **Teach them to handle failure** – Instead of giving up, they should learn from mistakes and keep going.
✔ **Help them set goals** – Teaching children to set and achieve goals builds motivation and discipline.

James 1:12 says:
"Blessed is the one who perseveres under trial because, having stood the test, that person will receive the crown of life that the Lord has promised to those who love Him."

Teaching perseverance helps children develop **resilience, determination, and faith in God's plan.**

6. Helping Children Understand the Connection Between Work and Rewards

The Bible teaches that **hard work brings rewards**:

- **Proverbs 14:23** – *"All hard work brings a profit, but mere talk leads only to poverty."*
- **2 Thessalonians 3:10** – *"The one who is unwilling to work shall not eat."*

Children should learn that **effort leads to reward**.

■ **Teach them the value of earning** – Instead of giving allowances freely, tie them to completed chores or good habits.

■ **Help them set financial goals** – Encourage saving, giving, and responsible spending.

■ **Show them the impact of their work** – Let them see how their contributions help the family and others.

Understanding the **connection between effort and rewards** helps children develop **motivation, responsibility, and gratitude**.

Teaching children **responsibility and a strong work ethic** is one of the most valuable gifts a father can give.

A father who **models hard work, sets expectations, and instills perseverance** prepares his children to succeed in life and honor God in all they do.

Key Takeaways:

■ **Work is a biblical principle** – Teach children that work is a way to serve and honor God.
■ **Children learn best from example** – A father's work ethic shapes his children's attitude toward responsibility.
■ **Giving responsibilities early builds confidence** – Age-appropriate tasks teach discipline and accountability.
■ **Excellence matters** – Encourage children to do their best in everything they undertake.
■ **Perseverance leads to success** – Help children develop resilience and determination.
■ **Hard work brings rewards** – Teach them that effort leads to meaningful accomplishments.

A father's role is not just to **provide for his family**, but to **prepare his children for life**. By raising **responsible, hardworking children**, he leaves a legacy of diligence, faithfulness, and honor to God.

Biblical Lessons on Stewardship and Money Management

One of the most crucial responsibilities a father has is to **teach his children the biblical principles of stewardship and money management**. In a world where financial irresponsibility leads to stress, debt, and poor life choices, equipping children with a **God-centered approach to finances** will set them up for a stable and fulfilling future.

The Bible provides clear guidance on **how to manage money wisely**, emphasizing **stewardship, contentment, generosity, and diligence.**

1. Understanding Biblical Stewardship

Stewardship means managing resources—money, time, talents, and possessions—according to God's principles. Children must learn that **everything belongs to God**, and they are simply **managers of His blessings.**

Key Scriptures on Stewardship:
■ **Psalm 24:1** – *"The earth is the Lord's, and everything in it, the world, and all who live in it."*
■ **1 Corinthians 4:2** – *"Now it is required that those who have been given a trust must prove faithful."*

■ **Luke 16:10** – *"Whoever can be trusted with very little can also be trusted with much."*

2. Teaching Children How to Handle Money God's Way

Money is a tool that can be used for good or bad. Fathers must teach their children to be **wise financial stewards** who honor God with their resources.

- **Earning Money Through Hard Work**

Children should learn that money comes from **diligence and honest labor**, not entitlement.

  - Encourage **chores, part-time jobs, and entrepreneurial efforts**.
  - Teach them the principle of **"working for what they have"** (2 Thessalonians 3:10).

- **The Importance of Giving**

Children should be taught that **giving back to God and others** is a key part of financial responsibility.

  - Teach them to **tithe (Malachi 3:10)** and give to those in need.
  - Show them how generosity **blesses both the giver and receiver** (Acts 20:35).

- **Saving and Delayed Gratification**

In a culture of **instant gratification**, children must learn the **value of patience** and saving.

- Proverbs 21:20 – *"The wise store up choice food and olive oil, but fools gulp theirs down."*
- Encourage them to **set financial goals and save for the future**.
- Teach the **difference between needs and wants**.

- **Avoiding Debt and Living Within Means**

Debt is one of the biggest financial traps. Teach children to **live within their means and avoid unnecessary borrowing**.

- **Proverbs 22:7** – *"The borrower is slave to the lender."*
- Help them understand **contentment and financial discipline**.

By grounding children in **biblical money management**, fathers prepare them to make **wise financial decisions as adults**.

Preparing Kids for Adulthood with Life Skills

A father's role goes beyond teaching faith and work ethic—it also includes **equipping children with essential life skills** to navigate adulthood successfully. Many young adults struggle because they were never taught **basic responsibilities and practical knowledge.**

Proverbs 22:6 – *"Train up a child in the way he should go, and when he is old he will not depart from it."*

1. Teaching Personal Responsibility

One of the most critical life skills is **personal responsibility**—understanding that actions have consequences and taking ownership of choices.

✔ **Teach accountability** – Children must learn that mistakes are opportunities to grow, not excuses to blame others.
✔ **Encourage decision-making** – Give them opportunities to make choices and experience the results.
✔ **Model responsibility** – Show them how to admit mistakes, correct them, and move forward.

2. Practical Life Skills Every Child Should Learn

Fathers should **actively teach and guide** their children in practical skills that will prepare them for independence. Here are key areas to focus on:

- **Time Management and Organization**

    - Teach children to **plan their day, set priorities, and avoid procrastination**.
    - Encourage the use of **calendars, to-do lists, and schedules**.
    - Show them the importance of **being punctual and keeping commitments**.

- **Basic Home Management Skills**

    - Cooking simple, nutritious meals.
    - Doing laundry and organizing personal spaces.
    - Cleaning and maintaining a home responsibly.

- **Financial Independence**

    - Budgeting and tracking expenses.
    - Understanding credit, interest, and responsible spending.
    - Paying bills and managing bank accounts.

- **Effective Communication and Conflict Resolution**

- Teach children how to express themselves **clearly, respectfully, and confidently.**
- Guide them in resolving conflicts **without aggression or avoidance.**
- Show them the power of **active listening and patience.**

* **Problem-Solving and Critical Thinking**

  - Encourage children to **think through challenges logically.**
  - Let them **solve small problems on their own** instead of always stepping in.
  - Teach them how to **analyze situations, weigh options, and make wise decisions.**

* **Basic Car and Home Maintenance**

  - Checking oil, tire pressure, and car maintenance basics.
  - Fixing minor household repairs.
  - Understanding the value of taking care of possessions.

By **gradually teaching these skills,** fathers ensure that their children **transition smoothly into responsible adulthood.**

Raising Future Leaders with Wisdom and Faith

Fathers have a **God-given responsibility** to raise children who are **hardworking, responsible, and equipped for adulthood**. This is not just about preparing them for careers—it's about shaping them into individuals who **serve God faithfully, manage their lives wisely, and contribute positively to society**.

Key Takeaways:

■ **Biblical Stewardship Matters** – Teach children that everything belongs to God, and they are **managers, not owners**.
■ **Work Ethic and Money Management Are Connected** – Instill a **strong work ethic, discipline, and financial wisdom**.
■ **Personal Responsibility Builds Maturity** – Help children **understand consequences, take accountability, and make wise choices**.
■ **Life Skills Prepare Children for Adulthood** – Teach **budgeting, time management, problem-solving, and independence**.

As Proverbs 14:23 states:
"All hard work brings a profit, but mere talk leads only to poverty."

By raising children who **work hard, manage resources wisely, and live with integrity**, fathers set them up for a **life of success, service, and faithfulness to God.**

Chapter 8

Passing Down a Legacy of Faith

A father's role extends beyond providing, protecting, and disciplining—he is also a **spiritual guide**, entrusted with the responsibility of **passing down a legacy of faith**. The values, beliefs, and principles a father models and teaches will shape not only his children's lives but also the generations to come.

The Bible speaks clearly about the **influence of a father's faithfulness**:

Deuteronomy 6:6-7 – *"These commandments that I give you today are to be on your hearts. Impress them on your children. Talk about them when you sit at home and when you walk along the road, when you lie down and when you get up."*

This passage emphasizes that faith is not just **taught**—it is **lived out daily**. Children learn about God **not only through words but through the consistent example set by their fathers**.

The Impact of a Father's Example

A father's faith, character, and integrity **leave a lasting imprint** on his children. Studies and biblical teachings show that **children are more likely to embrace Christianity when they see their father genuinely living out his faith.**

1. A Father's Life Is His Greatest Sermon

Children are incredibly observant. They may not always listen to what their father says, but they will **always watch what he does**. A father's **actions, decisions, and responses to life's challenges** teach children more about faith than any sermon ever could.

- **Leading by Example in Faith**

    - A father who **prays regularly** teaches his children to rely on God in all circumstances.
    - A father who **reads and studies the Bible** shows his children that God's Word is essential.
    - A father who **treats others with love, kindness, and integrity** models Christ-like behavior.

- **How a Father Handles Adversity**

Life is full of trials, and children closely observe **how their father responds to difficulties**.

- Does he trust God in times of uncertainty, or does he panic and complain?
- Does he forgive those who wrong him, or does he hold grudges?
- Does he demonstrate **peace and faith** in the face of hardships?

Children will imitate **what they see** in their father's life. If they see him **turn to God in all situations**, they will learn to do the same.

---

2. The Role of a Father in Spiritual Leadership

The Bible calls fathers to be **spiritual leaders in the home**, guiding their children toward **a deep, personal relationship with God**.

- **Joshua's Commitment as a Father**

Joshua 24:15 – *"As for me and my household, we will serve the Lord."*

- Joshua **took spiritual responsibility for his home** and set a clear direction for his family.

- Every father should be able to say the same, ensuring that **faith is a priority in the household.**

♦ **Priestly Responsibility in the Home**

A godly father acts as the **priest of his family**, leading them in prayer, worship, and the study of God's Word.

- He should **pray for and with his children regularly.**
- He should ensure that **biblical values are upheld** in the home.
- He should **encourage his children to develop their own relationship with God.**

When a father **takes spiritual leadership seriously**, his children will be more likely to **remain strong in faith throughout their lives.**

---

3. Demonstrating Love, Grace, and Forgiveness

One of the most powerful ways a father passes down faith is by **showing unconditional love, grace, and forgiveness**, just as Christ does.

- **Children Learn God's Love Through Their Father's Love**

  - A child who **feels loved by his father** will understand the love of God more easily.
  - A father's **patience, kindness, and compassion** reflect the heart of God.
  - Fathers must be intentional about **expressing love verbally and through actions**.

- **Teaching Grace and Forgiveness**

  - Just as God forgives, fathers must teach their children to **forgive others and seek reconciliation**.
  - A father who apologizes when he makes mistakes teaches **humility and the power of grace**.

The **love of a father** lays the foundation for children to **embrace and understand God's unconditional love**.

---

4. Passing Down Biblical Values and Traditions

Children need to see faith **practiced daily, not just on Sundays**. Fathers must establish **godly routines and traditions** in the home.

- **Prioritizing Family Devotions and Bible Study**
  - Set aside time each day for **prayer, reading Scripture, and discussing biblical principles.**
  - Encourage children to **ask questions and explore their faith.**

- **Celebrating Christian Milestones Together**
  - Observing holidays like **Christmas and Easter with a focus on Christ.**
  - Encouraging participation in **baptism, communion, and church involvement.**

- **Teaching the Importance of Serving Others**
  - Engage children in **acts of kindness, charity, and community service.**
  - Show them that **faith is lived out through serving God and others.**

When faith is **woven into daily life**, children develop **a deep-rooted love for God** that lasts into adulthood.

Leaving a Lasting Spiritual Legacy

A father's faith does not just affect his immediate family—it impacts **future generations**. When a man **lives a life of faith, obedience, and devotion to God**, he sets a foundation for **his children, grandchildren, and beyond**.

Key Takeaways:

■ **A father's example is his most powerful teaching tool.** Children learn faith by watching how their father lives.

■ **Spiritual leadership in the home is essential.** Fathers must **pray, teach, and guide their children toward God**.

■ **Love, grace, and forgiveness reflect God's heart.** Children who experience their father's love **better understand God's love**.

■ **Faith must be an active part of daily life.** Biblical teachings, traditions, and service to others **help faith take root**.

■ **A godly father leaves a spiritual legacy.** The faith he builds in his children **will be carried on for generations**.

Psalm 103:17-18 – *"But from everlasting to everlasting the Lord's love is with those who fear him, and his righteousness with their children's children—with those who keep his covenant and remember to obey his precepts."*

A father's **greatest success is not in material wealth but in passing down a strong, unwavering faith** that will endure for generations.

A father's greatest gift to his children is not wealth, property, or social status—it is **a strong spiritual foundation** that will guide them through life and into eternity. Leaving behind a spiritual inheritance and raising the next generation of godly leaders requires intentionality, faithfulness, and unwavering commitment to biblical principles.

How to Leave a Spiritual Inheritance

A spiritual inheritance is **the faith, wisdom, and values** passed down from one generation to the next. Unlike material wealth, which can be lost or misused, a spiritual inheritance has **eternal value** and will shape the lives of future generations.

Proverbs 13:22 says:
"A good man leaves an inheritance to his children's children, but the sinner's wealth is laid up for the righteous."

This verse reminds us that the legacy we leave should not only be financial but **spiritual and moral**, guiding our children toward **a lifelong walk with God**.

1. Prioritizing God's Word in the Home

The first step in leaving a spiritual inheritance is ensuring that **God's Word is the foundation of family life**. Children should grow up seeing the Bible **not just as a religious book, but as the ultimate source of wisdom, guidance, and truth.**

- **Ways to Prioritize God's Word:**

  - Read the Bible together daily as a family.
  - Encourage children to memorize key Scriptures.
  - Apply biblical lessons to everyday situations.
  - Use family discussions to reinforce biblical principles.

Deuteronomy 6:6-7 emphasizes this:
"These commandments that I give you today are to be on your hearts. Impress them on your children. Talk about them when you sit at home and when you walk along the road, when you lie down and when you get up."

By making **God's Word a daily part of life**, children learn to depend on it **as their ultimate guide**.

2. Living a Life of Faith and Obedience

A father's **example of faith** is the most powerful lesson his children will ever learn. It is **not enough to tell children to trust God**—they need to see their father **trust God in his own life**.

- **Practical Ways to Model Faith:**

    - Show **faith in action** by relying on God in difficult times.
    - Be **consistent in prayer, worship, and obedience** to God's commands.
    - Demonstrate **honesty, integrity, and humility** in all areas of life.
    - Seek forgiveness when mistakes are made and **show the power of grace**.

When children see their father **living out his faith daily**, they are more likely to embrace it as their own.

---

3. Teaching the Value of Service and Generosity

Jesus taught that **serving others** is one of the greatest ways to live out faith. A father should instill in his children the importance of **loving and helping others**.

- **Ways to Teach a Heart of Service:**

  - Volunteer as a family in church or community outreach.
  - Support those in need through giving and acts of kindness.
  - Encourage children to use their **gifts and talents for God's work**.

Acts 20:35 reminds us:
"It is more blessed to give than to receive."

When children grow up seeing their father **serve others with joy and generosity**, they learn that **faith is about more than just words—it's about action.**

---

4. Establishing Family Traditions that Reinforce Faith

Family traditions help reinforce a spiritual inheritance by creating **consistent and meaningful practices** that bring faith into everyday life.

- **Faith-Based Family Traditions:**

  - **Daily prayer and devotionals** before meals or bedtime.
  - **Attending church together** as a family.

- **Celebrating Christian holidays** with a focus on Jesus.
- **Keeping a gratitude journal** to encourage thankfulness.

Psalm 145:4 says:
"One generation shall commend your works to another, and shall declare your mighty acts."

Faith-based traditions **strengthen family unity and build a deep-rooted faith** that children will carry into their own homes one day.

---

5. Praying Over Your Children and Future Generations

One of the most powerful ways to leave a spiritual inheritance is by **praying for your children daily**. A father's prayers are **a spiritual covering** that protects and guides his family.

- **Ways to Pray for Your Children:**
  - Pray for **their salvation and relationship with God**.
  - Pray for **wisdom, protection, and godly friendships**.
  - Pray for **their future spouse and family**.

- Pray for **their calling and purpose in life**.

James 5:16 says:
"The prayer of a righteous person is powerful and effective."

A father's prayers **outlive him** and continue to impact his children **long after he is gone**.

Raising the Next Generation of Godly Leaders

A father's role does not stop at **teaching faith**—he must also prepare his children to become **leaders who will carry their faith into the world**.

1 Timothy 4:12 encourages young believers:
"Let no one despise you for your youth, but set the believers an example in speech, in conduct, in love, in faith, in purity."

Fathers must **equip their children** to be leaders in their homes, churches, and communities.

1. Teaching Leadership Through Responsibility

Leadership begins with **learning responsibility**. Children need to be **given opportunities to lead**, make decisions, and take responsibility for their actions.

- ❖ **Ways to Teach Responsibility:**

  - Assign **age-appropriate chores and tasks** at home.
  - Encourage **decision-making and problem-solving**.
  - Teach them **the consequences of actions**—both good and bad.

When children learn **responsibility at home**, they are better equipped to become **strong leaders in the future**.

---

2. Encouraging Boldness and Courage

Godly leaders must be **bold in their faith** and stand for truth, even when it is difficult. Fathers must teach their children **to be courageous and unwavering** in their beliefs.

Joshua 1:9 declares:

"Be strong and courageous. Do not be afraid; do not be discouraged, for the Lord your God will be with you wherever you go."

- **Ways to Instill Courage in Children:**

  - Encourage them to **speak up for what is right**.
  - Teach them to **trust God in all situations**.
  - Help them understand that **challenges are opportunities for growth**.

A child who **learns courage from his father** will grow into a leader who stands firm in faith.

---

3. Equipping Children with Biblical Wisdom

A godly leader must be guided by **wisdom and discernment**. Fathers must teach their children how to **seek God's wisdom in all things**.

- **Teaching Biblical Wisdom:**

  - Encourage them to **read Proverbs for practical wisdom**.
  - Teach them to **pray before making decisions**.
  - Discuss **real-life challenges through a biblical lens**.

James 1:5 reminds us:
"If any of you lacks wisdom, let him ask God, who gives generously to all without reproach, and it will be given to him."

When children learn to seek **God's wisdom**, they are prepared to **lead with integrity and faith**.

A Legacy That Lasts for Generations

A father's greatest impact is not measured by **his career, achievements, or wealth**, but by the **faith he instills in his children**. The decisions made today will **shape the future of generations to come**.

- ■ **Prioritize God's Word and faith in the home.**
- ■ **Live out faith as an example for your children.**
- ■ **Teach responsibility, courage, and leadership.**
- ■ **Pray for and with your children daily.**
- ■ **Build strong family traditions centered on God.**

Psalm 112:1-2 promises:
"Blessed is the man who fears the Lord, who finds great delight in his commands. His children will be mighty in the land; the generation of the upright will be blessed."

May every father rise to the challenge of **leaving behind a legacy of faith that will last for generations to come**.

Conclusion

Embracing Your Role as a Godly Father

Fatherhood is one of the greatest callings a man can receive. It is a sacred responsibility that requires love, patience, wisdom, and, most importantly, faith in God. Throughout this book, we have explored the key aspects of **biblical fatherhood**—from raising children with discipline and love to instilling responsibility, leadership, and spiritual values that will last for generations.

As we conclude, let us reflect on the journey of fatherhood, commit to a lifetime of faithful parenting, and trust God in every step.

Reflecting on the Journey of Fatherhood

Fatherhood is a journey—one filled with **joys, challenges, and moments of deep learning**. Each stage of a child's life presents new lessons for both the child and the father. Looking back, a godly father should see his role as more than just a provider or disciplinarian. He is called to be a **spiritual leader, mentor, and protector** of his home.

1. Recognizing the Impact of a Father's Role

A father's words, actions, and faith have a **lasting influence** on his children. A child who grows up with a father who prays with him, teaches him the Word, and models godly character will carry those lessons into adulthood. Proverbs 22:6 states:
"Train up a child in the way he should go, and when he is old, he will not depart from it."

Fathers are planting seeds of faith and wisdom **every day**—in their discipline, in their encouragement, and in the way they love their family. Those seeds will **bear fruit in due time**.

- **Questions for Reflection:**

  - Have I been intentional in leading my children spiritually?
  - Do my children see Christ in the way I treat their mother and others?
  - Am I creating an atmosphere of love, respect, and open communication in my home?

- How can I improve as a godly father in the days ahead?

Taking time to reflect allows a father to **learn from his mistakes, celebrate his successes, and move forward with renewed purpose.**

---

2. Learning from Failures and Growing in Grace

No father is perfect. There will be times of **mistakes, shortcomings, and regrets**. But godly fatherhood is **not about perfection—it is about faithfulness**. A father who is willing to acknowledge his failures, seek forgiveness, and grow in grace **sets a powerful example for his children.**

- **Encouragement for Fathers Who Struggle:**
  - **God's grace is sufficient**—you are never beyond His help.
  - **Your past mistakes do not define you**—you can start anew.
  - **Children value love and presence more than perfection**—keep showing up.
  - **It is never too late to become the father God wants you to be.**

Psalm 103:13 reminds us:
"As a father has compassion on his children, so the Lord has compassion on those who fear him."

Just as **God is patient with us**, we must be patient with ourselves as we strive to **grow in our role as fathers**.

Committing to a Lifetime of Faithful Parenting

Fatherhood does not end when a child turns 18 or leaves home. A father's **role as a mentor, guide, and prayer warrior continues throughout his life.**

1. Being a Constant Source of Guidance and Support

As children grow into adulthood, they will face **new challenges—career choices, relationships, marriage, parenting, and faith struggles.** A father should remain **a steady and wise presence** in his children's lives.

- ◆ **Ways to Stay Involved as a Father:**
  - **Pray for your children daily, even when they are adults.**
  - **Offer guidance without controlling their choices.**

- Encourage them in their faith and responsibilities.
- Be present for major life milestones and transitions.

By remaining **a source of godly counsel**, a father ensures that his children will always have **a strong anchor to return to.**

---

2. Investing in Future Generations

A father's influence **extends beyond his own children.** He has the opportunity to **shape future generations**—his grandchildren, nephews, church community, and young men who look up to him.

Psalm 78:4 says:
"We will not hide them from their children, but tell to the coming generation the glorious deeds of the Lord, and his might, and the wonders that he has done."

- **Ways to Impact Future Generations:**
  - Be an active role model in your grandchildren's lives.
  - Mentor young men in church and the community.
  - Share your testimony of faith with others.
  - Live a life that inspires others to follow Christ.

A godly father leaves **not just a name, but a legacy of faith that echoes for generations.**

Trusting God in Every Step

Fatherhood is not an easy task. There will be **moments of doubt, worry, and challenges** that feel overwhelming. But no father is called to walk this journey alone. **God is the ultimate Father, and He is always present to give strength, wisdom, and guidance.**

1. Surrendering the Journey to God

One of the greatest lessons a father can learn is **to trust God completely** with his children. **There will be times when discipline feels ineffective, when prayers seem unanswered, or when a child makes choices that break a father's heart.** In these moments, **faith is essential.**

- ♦ **Ways to Trust God in Fatherhood:**
    - Pray **without ceasing** for your children.
    - Believe that **God is working in their lives,** even when you don't see it.

- Release anxiety and fear, knowing that **God loves your children even more than you do.**
- Stand on the promises of God, such as Isaiah 41:10:
  "Fear not, for I am with you; be not dismayed, for I am your God; I will strengthen you, I will help you, I will uphold you with my righteous right hand."

A father's **deepest peace** comes when he surrenders his children to **the perfect Father—God Himself.**

---

2. Walking in Faith, Not Fear

In a world filled with **challenges, distractions, and ungodly influences**, it is easy to parent from a place of fear. But godly fathers are called to **lead with faith**.

- **Encouragement for Fathers:**
  - Do not fear the future—**God is already there**.
  - Do not fear failure—**God's grace covers your mistakes**.
  - Do not fear the influence of the world—**God's power is greater**.
  - Do not fear losing your children—**Train them up in faith, and trust God with their journey**.

2 Timothy 1:7 reminds us:
"For God has not given us a spirit of fear, but of power, and of love, and of a sound mind."

A godly father **chooses faith over fear**—every single day.

Final Words: The Reward of Faithful Fatherhood

Fatherhood is **not just a duty—it is a calling and a privilege**. A man who raises his children in **the fear of the Lord** will see **the fruit of his labor**, both in this life and in eternity.

Proverbs 20:7 declares:
"The righteous who walks in his integrity—blessed are his children after him!"

A father who **walks with God**, leads with wisdom, and prays with faith will leave **a legacy that outlives him**.

- ◼ **Commit to being a godly father every day.**
- ◼ **Trust in God's strength and guidance.**
- ◼ **Love your children with Christ's love.**
- ◼ **Pass down a spiritual inheritance that will last forever.**

May every father embrace his calling with **courage, faith, and unwavering trust in God. The impact of a godly father lasts for generations.**

Made in the USA
Columbia, SC
25 May 2025